THE
BOOK
OF
HEAVEN

BY HARVEY MINKOFF, PH.D.

TESTAMENT
BOOKS

This 2001 edition is published by Testament Books™,
an imprint of Random House Value Publishing, Inc.
280 Park Avenue, New York, NY 10017
by arrangement with Ottenheimer Publishers, Inc.
5 Park Center Court, Suite 300, Owings Mills, MD 21117.

Testament Books™ and design are trademarks of
Random House Value Publishing, Inc.

Random House
New York • Toronto • London • Sydney • Auckland
http://www.randomhouse.com/

Printed and bound in the United States of America.

A catalog record for this title is available from the Library of Congress.

ISBN: 0-517-16405-1

9 8 7 6 5 4 3 2 1

CONTENTS

INTRODUCTION

WHAT IS HEAVEN?

Heaven is a place, a reward, a promise—an idea. Moses says, "I lift up my hand to heaven" in prayer (Deut. 32:40). Jesus tells his disciples to pray to "Our Father which art in heaven" (Matt. 6:9). We do good deeds in order to "lay up. . . treasures in heaven" (Matt. 6:20). And in the messianic era at the end of time, God will create "a new heaven and a new earth" (Isa. 65:17, Rev. 21:1).

From ancient times to the present, people have been fascinated and puzzled by the idea of heaven: What does heaven look like? What happens there? How do you get to heaven? Who lives there? Because the concept of an afterlife is central to so many religions and faiths, there are many different answers to these questions. Even people who don't believe in heaven probably have an image of what heaven must be like!

In this book, we will look at a wide range of ideas about heaven. We will see what the Bible has to say about heaven and hell, and we will review the thoughts of many scholars, philosophers, and poets. We'll see what people said about heaven in the past, and what part heaven plays in our lives today. Indeed, this book will try to answer all of your questions about heaven.

But first, we need to look at the actual word *heaven*. What do people mean when they use the word *heaven*? How is it used, in the Bible and other religious writings, to depict a place we can only imagine? As we will see, heaven can mean many different things, since language changes over time and according to who uses it.

First of all, *heaven* is the English word for an idea shared by many cultures, present and past. Ancient Egyptians, Babylonians, and Zoroastrians believed in "heaven." Native Americans, Jews, Christians, and Moslems believe in it too. However, views of what heaven is vary widely. And many people use the word *heaven* to talk about places or ideas that are not strictly what *heaven* means in this book.

The idea of heaven exists in many cultures and religions. It may include or overlap with ideas about paradise, the afterlife, immortality, resurrection, judgment, and the end of time. The many different understandings of heaven come into play, not only when we compare ancient Egyptian religion to modern Episcopalianism, but even when we look at the ideas of theologians within the same religious tradition. Even in the Bible itself, *heaven* can refer to any number of things: the sky, the abode of God, the reward of the righteous, the end of time, even to God himself. We will discuss all of these variations in this book.

Any discussion of heaven begins with a basic problem: How do we use human language to describe something in another dimension, something beyond the world of human senses? In addition, most descriptions of heaven, in Judeo-Christian and other traditions, are not in English. Whether the English word *heaven* appears in a particular translation is often only a matter of style.

And different translators may use a variety of English words—*sky, firmament, heaven, paradise, afterlife, world to come*—to translate Hebrew, Greek, or Latin writings. Even the same translators may vary their usage from sentence to sentence, omitting the word *heaven* when they're clearly talking about the idea of heaven. We'll look at these cases also in this book.

Sometimes, a translator inadvertently makes a foreign idea seem familiar by using a well-known English word. This often happens with the word that represents the opposite of *heaven*—*hell*. In the King James Version of the Bible, the word *hell* is used to translate two Hebrew words—*Sheol* and *Gehenna*—and two Greek words—*Hades* and *Tartaros*—which are different from each other. These instances are also included in this book.

On the other hand, the English word *heaven* is used in many phrases and idioms that are simply figures of speech, for example *hog heaven, heavens to Betsy,* a *heavenly smile.* The same is also true, of course, of the word *hell.* But, unless such metaphors are connected to a religious idea or reference, we won't go into them here.

How are metaphors important to our discussion of heaven? Moses Maimonides, the great twelfth-century philosopher and Bible scholar, argued that *all* references to God are figures of speech. After all, since God is not a material being, expressions like "God's hand" (Exod. 7:4–5, 15:6) *must* be metaphors. But Maimonides goes even further. Given that speech, hearing, and sight are all physically produced sensations, and given that God does not have physical organs, membranes, and nerves, it follows that God does not actually speak, hear, or see—at least in human terms. To say that God *spoke,* or *heard,* or *saw* are all, Maimonides writes, examples of metaphor.

In addition, much of the Bible is poetry. We're not talking about rhymed ditties, of course, but about some of the most exalted language and images in all of Western literature. The great prophets and teachers of the Bible captivated the minds of their audiences through many unforgettable word pictures:

God carries his people "on eagles' wings" (Exod. 19:4); the righteous will be "as a tree planted by the waters" (Jer. 17:8); pointless actions are like casting "pearls before swine" (Matt. 7:6).

Keeping this poetic language in mind, we might ask which references to heaven are actually figures of speech. For example, did the ancient Hebrews believe literally that rain poured out through "the windows of heaven" (Gen. 7:11)? Perhaps they did. But do we believe literally that the sun rises? When the author of Job said, "The pillars of heaven tremble" (Job 26:11), it is certainly possible that he believed, as so many ancients did, that heaven was actually supported on pillars. But he also said in the same passage (26:7) that the earth "hangeth. . .upon nothing," when most of his contemporaries thought it stood on pillars in the sea.

Obviously, there are no easy answers to these questions. While many such passages are quoted in this book, it's up to you as the reader to decide which are literal and which seem more like figures of speech.

CHAPTER ONE

WHAT ARE SOME FACTS ABOUT HEAVEN?

HOW MANY HEAVENS ARE THERE?

The Bible frequently talks about *heavens*, in the plural: "These are the generations of the heavens and of the earth" (Gen. 2:4). "Give ear, O ye heavens, and I will speak" (Deut. 32:1). "The heavens declare the glory of God" (Psalm 19:1). There are seven heavens in the main Judeo-Christian and Islamic traditions, each one better than the last. Hence, the expression for extreme happiness, "seventh heaven." Some ancient Christian books mention three heavens. In the astronomy of Ptolemy, the second-century Greek astronomer, and his followers, there are ten.

According to Ptolemaic theory, which held sway in Europe for over 1300 years, earth is the center of the universe. Ten heavenly spheres, or heavens, revolve around the earth in a complex system of connected circles. Starting outward from the earth, the first seven heavens correspond to the planets: Moon, Mercury, Venus, Sun, Mars, Jupiter, Saturn. The eighth heaven is the firmament containing the stars; the ninth is the crystalline sphere that controls the equinoxes. The tenth heaven is the seat of the primum mobile, the "prime mover" or "first moving thing" that provides the energy of the universe. This is the limit of the created world. Beyond it lies the empyrean—the fiery realm of the divine.

10	9	8	7	6
(primum mobile	(crystalline sphere	(firmament	(Saturn	(Jupiter

5	4	3	2	1	
(Mars	(Sun	(Venus	(Mercury	(Moon	(Earth)

In the Apocalypse of Paul, a very popular early Christian book that Augustine condemned as a forgery, the author speaks of three heavens. Accompanied by an angel, he is allowed to see the torment of sinners, the bliss of the righteous, and the hosts of angels praising God.

Another apocryphal work, the Book of the Secrets of Enoch (also called II Enoch and the Slavonic Enoch because of an important medieval translation of this work from the Greek) gives a vivid and detailed picture of the seven heavens as some Jews and first-century Christians understood them. The narrator is supposedly the biblical figure Enoch, who, according to Genesis 5:24, ascended into heaven without dying. He was carried on an angel's wings through the seven heavens, which, according to the book, are stacked on top of each other like the stories of a building. In the first heaven, the narrator sees the angels who rule the stars and keep the storehouses of dew and snow. In the second heaven, he finds fallen angels being tortured in darkness. The third heaven is divided in two. On one side, the righteous enjoy their reward in a beautiful garden; on the other side, the wicked suffer great punishment. The fourth heaven contains the wheels that rotate the sun, moon, stars, and winds. The fifth heaven contains evil angels who instigate crimes. In the sixth heaven, the narrator hears the heavenly choir singing praise to God. In the seventh heaven, he is allowed to see the Divine Throne from afar.

Enoch's heavens look like this:

7   Divine Throne

_____

6   heavenly choir

_____

5   evil angels

_____

4   sun, moon, stars, winds

_____

3   reward and punishment

_____

2   fallen angels

_____

1   storehouses of dew and snow

_____

EARTH

A few isolated sentences in II Enoch mention ten heavens, but these are not described in detail as the seven are. Most scholars assume that these lines about ten heavens were added much later.

In Islam, the first heaven is made of silver, and holds the stars, which hang on golden chains. The second heaven is made of gold, and is home to Jesus and John the Baptist. In the third heaven, which is encrusted with pearl, the Angel Azrael records the names of everyone who is born or who dies. Enoch lives in the fourth heaven with the Angel of Tears. Aaron and the Avenging Angel live in the fifth heaven. Moses and the Guardian Angel of Heaven are in the sixth heaven. Abraham, along with some very large angels singing praises to Allah, resides in the seventh heaven. This last heaven is made of divine light, indescribable in human language.

The Islamic heavens look like this:

7   Abraham and angels singing

---

6   Moses and the Guardian Angel

---

5   Aaron and the Avenging Angel

---

4   Enoch and the Angel of Tears

---

3   The Angel Azrael

---

2   Jesus and John the Baptist

---

1   the stars

EARTH

IS HEAVEN FAR AWAY?

In the Bible, heaven often stands as a symbol of great distance: "They come from a far country, from the end of heaven" (Isa. 13:5). "Our brethren have discouraged our heart, saying, The people is greater and taller than we; the cities are great and walled up to heaven" (Deut. 1:28). "For as the heavens are higher than the earth, so are my ways higher than your ways, and my thoughts than your thoughts" (Isa. 55:9).

The idea of great distance also communicates heaven's inaccessibility: "For this commandment which I command thee this day, it is not hidden from thee, neither is it far off. It is not in heaven, that thou shouldest say, Who shall go up for us to heaven, and bring it unto us" (Deut. 30:11–12). "Though they climb up to heaven, thence will I bring them down" (Amos 9:2).

In his great religious epic *Paradise Lost*, John Milton describes the time when Satan was cast out of heaven into hell:

. . . from morn
To noon he fell, from noon to dewy eve,
A summer's day; and with the setting sun
Dropp'd from the Zenith. . . .

Others envision heaven a little bit closer to home. In *The Rubáiyát of Omar Khayyam*, Edward FitzGerald writes:

I sent my Soul through the Invisible,
Some letter of that After-life to spell:
And by and by my Soul return'd to me,
And answer'd "I Myself am Heav'n and Hell."

Sir Walter Scott writes in *The Lay of the Last Minstrel*:
Love rules the court, the camp, the grove,
And men below, and saints above;
For love is heaven, and heaven is love.

And the nineteenth-century American philosopher-poet George Santayana put it concisely: "Heaven is to be at peace with things."

WHAT IS THE EARLIEST MENTION OF HEAVEN IN ENGLISH?

The Anglo-Saxon tribes of England were converted from paganism to Christianity beginning in 597. The missionaries came from Rome and used Latin in their liturgy and correspondence. They also trained native clerics to read and write Latin, although English must have been used in sermons and for teaching. According to the *Oxford English Dictionary*, the earliest surviving written occurrences of the word *heaven* are in the poem *Beowulf*, composed in the first half of the eighth century. The word *heaven* appears ten times; this reference is the most interesting for our purposes:

. . . ne wiston hie Drihten God,
ne hie huru heofona Helm herian ne cuþon
This translates literally as:
. . . not knew they Lord God,
not they indeed heavens' Protector to praise not knew
In idiomatic English it is:
. . . they didn't know Lord God,
indeed they didn't know to praise the heavens' Protector

WHERE DO THE WORDS HEAVEN AND HELL COME FROM?

The words *heaven* and *hell* have existed in English for as long as we have had written records of the language, that is, for more than twelve hundred years. However, before the Anglo-Saxon tribes were converted to Christianity, the words *heaven* and *hell* did not have their current religious meanings. They acquired these meanings when missionaries and teachers tried to find native words to explain the concepts of Christianity.

The word heaven can be traced back to an Old English, or Anglo-Saxon, word variously spelled *heben*, *hefen*, and *heofon*. Originally, the word seems to have meant the expanse containing the sun, moon, and stars. In the eighth-century poem *Beowulf*, for example, the sun is called "heaven's candle."

Hell is from an ancient root meaning "cover, hide." In Teutonic mythology, *Hel* (or *hell*, *hille*, or *halja*) is the shadowy home of the dead. In Norse myth, *Hel* eventually came to be the name of the goddess in charge of this region. The word *hell* and the native concepts attached to it were easily adapted to Christian use when the Anglo-Saxons converted to Christianity.

WHAT ARE SOME OTHER NAMES FOR HEAVEN AND HELL?

The most common English synonyms for heaven are *paradise* and *sky*. The first describes the concept of blessedness;

11

the second refers to the physical place. In hymns and religious writings we also find many words and phrases for heaven: *Kingdom of God, Garden of Eden, Zion, Heavenly City, Celestial City, Canaan, New Canaan, Jerusalem, New Jerusalem,* and *Holy City.* Drawing on the mythology of Greece, Rome, and other cultures, English poetry often refers to heaven as *Elysium, Elysian fields, Empyrean, Valhalla, nirvana,* and *Happy Hunting Grounds.*

Some common synonyms for hell are *Sheol, Gehenna, Hades, Tartarus,* the *Underworld,* the *pit,* the *inferno,* and the *abyss.* Less common names are *pandemonium, Acheron, Abadon, Tophet, Stygian region,* and *Plutonic realm.*

IS PARADISE THE SAME AS HEAVEN?

Paradise is frequently used as a synonym for heaven, but it also refers to two other ideas.

The word *paradise* is from the Persian word *pairidaeze,* which originally meant a royal garden or enclosure. With this meaning, but pronounced *pardes,* it appears in the biblical Song of Songs 4:13, Ecclesiastes 2:5, and Nehemiah 2:8. After the Persian word was borrowed by the Greeks as *paradeisos,* it was used in Greek translations of the Bible to refer to the Garden of Eden in the story of Adam and Eve.

When Jewish and Christian thinkers elaborated on the idea of a home for the blessed in the afterlife, they used the word *paradise* in its various pronunciations. Sometimes they used *paradise* as a synonym for heaven and other times to designate a part of heaven. In 2 Enoch 8–9, for example, *paradise* is a place in the third level of heaven.

IS THE GARDEN OF EDEN IN HEAVEN?

In Genesis, the story of Adam and Eve (2:8–14) places the Garden of Eden somewhere in the Middle East, at the source of the Euphrates River:

> And the Lord God planted a garden eastward in Eden; and there he put the man whom he had formed. . . . And a river went out of Eden to water the garden; and from thence it was parted, and became into four heads. The name of the first is Pison. . . . And the name of the second river is Gihon: the same is it that encompasseth the whole land of Ethiopia. And the name of the third river is Hidekel: that is it which goeth toward the east of Assyria. And the fourth river is Euphrates.

In later Jewish thought, the earthly Garden of Eden was interpreted as a symbol for—or even a mirror of—a heavenly Garden of Eden. Describing the place of the righteous in the third heaven, 2 Enoch 8 says: "And two springs come out which send forth honey and milk . . . and they separate into four parts . . . and go down into the paradise of Eden, between corruptibility and incorruptibility. And thence they go forth along the earth. . . ."

In modern Jewish terminology, the phrase *Garden of Eden* (*Gan Eden* in Hebrew) embodies the idea of reward in a spiritual afterlife and thus comes closest to the idea of the English word *heaven.*

IS HEAVEN FOREVER?

According to many passages in the Bible, heaven will last for a very, very long time. In some passages, it is even presented as an image of eternity. In Matthew 24:35, Jesus says, "Heaven and earth shall pass away, but my words shall not pass away." And in Matthew 5:18 he says, "Till heaven and earth pass, one jot or one tittle shall in no wise pass from the law." Both passages imply, of course, that heaven will *not* pass away.

But in other places, the Bible says that heaven will not last forever, but will be replaced by a new, eternal heaven. Similarly, souls that go to the heaven that now exists will remain there until the new heaven, or resurrection, comes. After that, they too will become eternal.

The British romantic poet Percy Bysshe Shelley writes in *Adonis*:

The One remains, the many change and pass;
Heaven's light forever shines, Earth's shadows fly.

Throughout the ages, poets have used the concept of heaven to describe an unchanging, eternal place. Using the image of day becoming night, Christopher Wordsworth describes how the soul will eventually live in God's eternal light:

The day is gently sinking to a close,
Fainter and yet more faint the sunlight glows.
O Brightness of Thy Father's glory, Thou
Eternal Light of Light, be with us now.
Where Thou art present darkness cannot be.
Midnight is glorious noon, O Lord, with Thee.

Our changeful lives are ebbing to an end;
Onward to darkness and to death we tend.
O Conqueror of the grave, be Thou our guide,
Be Thou our light in death's dark eventide;
Then in our mortal hour will be no gloom,
No sting in death, no terror in the tomb.

The weary world is moldering to decay,
Its glories wane, its pageants fade away;
In that last sunset, when the stars shall fall,
May we arise, awakened by Thy call,
With Thee, O Lord, forever to abide
In that blest day which has no eventide.

WHAT IS THE NEW HEAVEN?

The culminating message of the prophet Isaiah, in chapters 65–66, refers to a new heaven. In a future messianic age, God will establish a new world order in which life will be radically transformed. The plain of Sharon will be a pasture for sheep; the valley of Achor a place for herds. The righteous shall have enough to eat and drink; they shall sing from the joy of their hearts. And then:

> He who blesseth himself in the earth shall bless himself in the God of truth; and he that sweareth in the earth shall swear by the God of truth; because the former troubles are forgotten, and because they are hid from mine eyes. For, behold, I create new heavens and a new earth: and the former shall not be remembered, nor come into mind. . . . for, behold, I create Jerusalem a rejoicing, and her people a joy. And I will rejoice in Jerusalem, and joy in my people. . . .

In this blessed age, God will answer prayers before they are even uttered, and peace will prevail everywhere:

And it shall come to pass, that before they call, I will answer; and while they are yet speaking, I will hear. The wolf and the lamb shall feed together, and the lion shall eat straw like the bullock; and dust shall be the serpent's meat. They shall not hurt nor destroy in all my holy mountain, saith the Lord.

Finally, unlike the present heaven, the new heaven will be eternal, as will God's covenant with His people: "For as the new heavens and the new earth, which I will make, shall remain before me, saith the Lord, so shall your seed and your name remain."

Here is a more detailed description of this new age from Revelation 21:

And I saw a new heaven and a new earth: for the first heaven and the first earth were passed away; and there was no more sea. . . . And God shall wipe away all tears from their eyes; and there shall be no more death, neither sorrow, nor crying, neither shall there be any more pain; for the former things are passed away. And he that sat upon the throne said, Behold, I make all things new. . . . And he said unto me, It is done. I am Alpha and Omega, the beginning and the end. I will give unto him that is athirst of the fountain of the water of life freely.

WHAT IS THE HEAVENLY CITY?

Describing the new heaven and new earth, Revelation 21 also speaks of a heavenly version of Jerusalem:

And there came unto me one of the seven angels . . . and shewed me that great city, the holy Jerusalem, descending out of heaven from God, Having the glory of God: and her light was like unto a stone most precious, even like a jasper stone, clear as crystal; And had a wall great and high, and had twelve gates, and at the gates twelve angels, and names written thereon, which are the names of the twelve tribes of the children of Israel. . . . And the twelve gates were twelve pearls: every several gate was of one pearl: and the street of the city was pure gold, as it were transparent glass. . . . And the city had no need of the sun, neither of the moon, to shine in it, for the glory of God did lighten it, and the Lamb is the light thereof.

WHO WENT TO HEAVEN WITHOUT DYING?

The Bible says clearly (II Kings 2:11) that, while he was talking to his disciple Elisha, the prophet Elijah ascended to heaven without dying:

And it came to pass, as they still went on, and talked, that, behold, there appeared a chariot of fire, and horses of fire, and parted them both asunder; and Elijah went up by a whirlwind into heaven. And Elisha saw it, and he cried, My father, my father, the chariot of Israel, and the horsemen thereof. And he saw him no more.

A more puzzling passage (Gen. 6:24) says that Enoch, the father of Methuselah, "walked with God: and he was not; for God took him." Traditionally, scholars interpret this to mean that Enoch went to heaven without dying. Hebrews 11:5 uses the term *translation* to describe this mysterious event: "By faith Enoch was translated that he should not see death; and was not found, because God had translated him: for before his translation he had this testimony, that he pleased God."

Judaism, Christianity, and Islam all contain legends about people who went to heaven without dying—for example, the daughter of Pharaoh who saved Moses; King Hiram of Tyre who helped Solomon build the temple in Jerusalem; Ebedmelech the Ethiopian who rescued the prophet Jeremiah.

According to Muslim tradition, the Dome of the Rock in Jerusalem encloses the sacred rock from which Mohammed ascended for a visionary tour of heaven. On another occasion, when it was reported that Mohammed had died, Mohammed's confidant Omar claimed that, like Moses, the prophet would return in forty days with a new message from God. Omar was rebuked by Abu Bakr, Mohammed's successor, who said: "Whoever worships Mohammed, know that Mohammed is dead. Whoever worships God, know that God is alive and immortal."

A Jewish legend (the story of Rabbi Ben Levi) was made famous by Henry Wadsworth Longfellow in *Tales of a Wayside Inn*. Familiar to generations of American schoolchildren, the poem begins:

Rabbi Ben Levi, on the Sabbath, read
A volume of the Law, in which it said,
"No man shall look upon my face and live."
And as he read, he prayed that God would give
His faithful servant grace with mortal eye
To look upon His face and yet not die.

CHAPTER TWO

WHO BELİEVES İN HEAVEN AND HELL?

WHO BELİEVES İN HEAVEN?

The three great monotheistic religions—Judaism, Christianity, and Islam—hold a common belief in reward and punishment in an afterlife. However, they differ widely in their understanding of heaven and hell. In addition, many other cultures and religions, both ancient and modern, teach of an afterlife or have beliefs that correspond to the idea of heaven and hell. Some philosophical systems and religions focus on this life and play down or deny life after death. Even among Jews, Christians, and Muslims there are those who don't consider heaven central to their religion.

More people in the United States believe in heaven and hell than in any other industrialized western country. Surveys show that about 85 percent of Americans answer "yes" to the question "Do you believe in heaven?" In Great Britain the number is about 55 percent, in Germany about 45 percent, and in France about 40 percent. While the surveys don't usually follow up by asking people to explain their idea of heaven, it's interesting that only about 75 percent of Americans say they believe in life after death, in other words, 10 percent fewer than those who believe in heaven. Only about 65 percent of Americans say they believe in hell, which shows that belief in heaven and belief in hell are not necessarily connected.

In the United States, the extent of belief in heaven is about the same among men and women, among people of different ages, among members of different Christian denominations, and among political liberals and conservatives. A major difference in numbers of believers emerges only when we come to education. While more than 90 percent of people with only a grade school education believe in heaven, only about 70 percent of college graduates do. Among the clergy, almost all Catholic priests express a belief in life after death, in contrast to about 85 percent of Protestant ministers.

WHAT DID ANCIENT CULTURES BELIEVE ABOUT HEAVEN?

Because our distant ancestors didn't leave written records, what knowledge we have of the earliest beliefs about the afterlife come from anthropology and archaeology.

Primitive cultures apparently believed that humans were supposed to be immortal. Death was unnatural—the result of angry spirits, carelessness, disobedience, or sorcery. Death from disease was clearly the result of evil spirits; death at the hands of an enemy meant that his magic was stronger; and death during the hunt was caused by the spirit of the hunted animal. Even death through old age could be explained as a loss of vigor caused by an enemy's sorcery or a god's anger. The obvious defense against death was to take greater care in performing magic, to obey the will of spirits, or simply to possess better spells, curses, and sorcery than one's enemy.

When death occurred, as it inevitably did, how ancient peoples handled the body reflected belief in an afterworld. Animals, of course, do not bury their dead; but for thousands of years, humans have. Why? Scholars believe that respect for the dead implies a belief that to be human means more than just possessing a physical body. Ancient religious or mystical beliefs are reflected in rituals like the practice of burying the body in a special position or in a special direction. And, certainly, burial sites that include tools, food, and favorite possessions prove that friends of the deceased felt that he or she was going to a place where these things would be appreciated. In Mesopotamia (modern Iraq) four-thousand-year-old tombs contain food, wine, furniture, jewelry, musical instruments, and weapons. Some even contain skeletons of courtiers, soldiers, and slaves who seem to have willingly gone along to serve their master in the afterlife.

Some cultures had medicine men who would help the soul leave the dead body, explain its new existence to it, show it the way to its new home, and protect the living from a possibly angry spirit that still wished to defend its former home and possessions. Feasts for the deceased and his or her friends might be held in the days preceding burial, at the tomb, or for a number of days afterward. All of these rituals show that the soul of the dead person was still considered a part of the community.

WHAT DİD THE ANCİENT EGYPTİANS BELİEVE?

Ancient Egyptians kept extensive written records about the afterlife. On the walls of tombs and pyramids more than four thousand years old, the Egyptians carved prayers to help the soul of the deceased reach the place of eternal bliss.

Some tombs even contain the Book of the Dead, which taught the spirit how to meet with Osiris, the god of immortality. Worshippers of Osiris believed that the soul (ba) and its guardian spirit (ka) could achieve immortality, as Osiris had done, if the physical body was mummified and the proper funeral rituals were followed. This afterlife was open to all worshippers. Pharaohs had the additional privilege of ascending to heaven in the chariot of Re, the sun-god. To determine if the soul of the deceased was worthy of its final reward, it had to prove to the forty-two judges of the dead that it had not committed the forty-two terrible sins. The messenger-god Anubis and the scribe-god Thoth then weighed the heart of the dead in the balance of truth to see whether it deserved reward or punishment in the afterworld.

Originally the Egyptians believed that the afterworld was in the sky, beyond the dome of heaven. Later, however, they believed that the dead went under the earth, where the sun went at night. Here the dead lived with the gods in beautiful gardens and homes.

HOW IS HEAVEN DEPICTED IN GREEK MYTHOLOGY?

Many of the tribes that settled in Europe shared related languages and myths. For example, the ancestral sky-god Dyeus was venerated as Zeus by the Greeks and as Jupiter by the Romans. Because of their early adoption of the alphabet, we can read the particularly full accounts of the afterlife left by Greek and Roman writers. Notably, they believed that all people go to the same Underworld—called *Hades* after its ruler—where some suffer and others enjoy happiness.

According to Greek myth, Hades abducted Persephone to make her queen of the Underworld. Persephone's mother, Demeter (Earth-Mother), went into mourning and stopped producing food for humankind. To prevent widespread famine, Zeus arranged for Persephone to visit her mother for eight months each year, leaving only the four months of winter for Demeter to mourn. Demeter's emergence from mourning each spring was marked by days of thanksgiving among the Greeks. Eventually, these springtime celebrations came to be seen as a way of making Persephone happy, and of ensuring better treatment in her Underworld domain.

Another god who came to life in the spring was Dionysos. His worship was often associated with orgies of eating, drinking, and sexuality. Later, however, these festivities incorporated aspects of the veneration of Orpheus, the musician who descended into Hades to bring back his beloved Eurydice. In this form, the cult of Orpheus became a means of learning the secrets of immortality and happiness in Hades.

In the *Odyssey*, Homer describes the hero Odysseus' descent into Hades. There he asks the all-knowing spirits why

23

he is being driven from place to place in the Mediterranean instead of being allowed to return home from the Trojan War. In Hades Odysseus meets the spirit of his mother, but when he tries to hug her, her physical body disintegrates. All that remains is an ethereal shade. To the Greeks, who gloried in the sensuous pleasures of the body, such a spiritual eternity was unhappy indeed.

Greek poets also speak of the Elysian fields, a place situated either in the Underworld or at the far western end of the earth. Here, there is neither snow nor storm, but only cool ocean breezes.

WHAT DOES ROMAN MYTHOLOGY SAY ABOUT HEAVEN?

With slight changes in names and details, Greek myths were also part of Roman religion. In the *Aeneid*, the great epic of imperial Rome, Virgil describes the visit of Aeneas, Trojan hero and founder of the city, to the Underworld.

At the shore of the River Styx, Aeneas sees Charon rowing spirits of the dead to the Underworld. Many thousands of spirits are left behind, milling around for centuries because their mortal bodies have not been properly buried. On the far shore Aeneas finds the spirits of infants, of the wrongly executed, and of suicides. Farther on, in the Fields of Mourning, those who died for love continue to pine. In the farthest field Aeneas sees warriors who died in battle. His Trojan comrades are happy to see Aeneas, but his Greek enemies make thin, hollow cries as they flee him.

Beyond this area the road forks. To the right, the path to Elysium awaits; to the left, a tunnel leads to Tartarus. Tartarus is surrounded by three huge walls and a burning river. Aeneas hears screams and moans behind the walls, and the sound of beatings and rattling chains. Here the spirits of the wicked are broken on spiked wheels, whipped with snakes, eaten by vultures, or made to roll a giant boulder up a hill—for all eternity. In contrast, the Elysian fields are resplendent with vegetation and bright light. Here the pious sing and dance, wrestle, and compete in sports. Nearby, their horses graze. Everything delightful in life is available here.

In the Underworld, Aeneas hears these wise words:

The descent to the Underworld is easy:
night and day the door stands open.
But to reverse your steps,
and reach the upper air—
that's work, that's labor.

WHAT DID THE ANGLO-SAXON TRIBES BELIEVE ABOUT HEAVEN?

The pagan Anglo-Saxons had a runic writing system used for inscriptions and, possibly, magic. However, all surviving documents in their language date from after their conversion to Christianity and reflect their new religion. Still, names of pagan gods can be found, like fossils, in modern English: for example, Woden in Wednesday (that is, Woden's day), Thor in Thursday, Freya in Friday. This suggests that the Anglo-Saxons shared the beliefs of other Germanic tribes, which are preserved in great detail in the Norse *Eddas*, which contain myths of Iceland.

According to these myths, the universe sits on a huge ash tree. At its foot sits Wyrd (Destiny), who controls human fate.

The first living being was a giant named Ymir. He was killed by his son Odin (Woden), who created the earth, Middangeard (Middle-yard), from Ymir's flesh and the sky from his skull. In Middangeard, but separated from human habitation by the bridge of the rainbow, is the place of the gods. Far to the north is Hel, the home of the dead.

Warriors slain in battle are taken by Valkyries (corpse-choosers) to Valhalla (corpse-hall), where they feast and carouse with Odin. They keep in shape through mock battles so that they will be ready to fight on Odin's side when the world ends at Ragnarok (Twilight of the Gods).

WHAT DOES JUDAISM TEACH ABOUT HEAVEN?

The Hebrew Bible—called the Old Testament in the Christian Bible—is sacred to Judaism, Christianity, and Islam. As we've seen, many beliefs about heaven and hell are shared by these three great monotheistic religions. All three teach that the soul is immortal and lives on after the death of the physical body. All three share the belief that the soul is judged after death for the actions of the living person, and that there are rewards and punishment in the afterlife.

The clearest statement in the Hebrew Bible concerning the afterlife is probably Daniel 12:2–3:

And many of them that sleep in the dust of the earth shall awake, some to everlasting life, and some to shame and everlasting contempt. And they that be wise shall shine as the brightness of the firmament; and they that turn many to righteousness as the stars for ever and ever.

Ideas about heaven and hell are more fully developed in Jewish writings other than the Hebrew Bible, some of which are included in the Catholic Bible and in the Protestant Apocrypha. The *Wisdom of Solomon*, for example, ridicules those who say that there is nothing after death. Rather, the author says, humankind does not perish, because we are made in the image of God. The holy will receive their reward, and only those who side with the devil will suffer true death.

The usual terms in Judaism for heaven are *Gan Eden* ("Garden of Eden") and *Olam Ha-bah* ("The World to Come"). As one great rabbi says in the section of the *Talmud* called "Ethics of the Fathers":

> This world is an anteroom to the world to come. Prepare yourself in the anteroom so that you may enter into the inner chamber. One hour of spiritual calm in the world to come is better than all of life in this world.

Despite some references in ancient sources to banquets and physical pleasures in the afterlife, Jewish religious thinkers have not generally invested much effort in describing heaven. And modern Jewish teachers tend to interpret those descriptions that do exist as poetic images—attempts to describe the indescribable. According to modern Jewish ideas of heaven, souls find spiritual pleasure in the presence of God. As Maimonides explained, since neither God nor souls have material substance, it follows that they don't need a "place" to gather. Heaven is simply this state of pleasure in enjoying God.

Modern Judaism includes a concept called *Gehinnom*, which is written as *Gehenna* in Christian sources and is often translated as *hell*. But the Jewish *Gehinnom* is quite different from the Christian and Islamic hell. Unlike Christianity and Islam, Judaism does not teach that wicked souls suffer eternal pain in hell. Rather, souls that are not ready or worthy to enjoy the presence of God are cleansed in *Gehinnom*—as in the fire of a kiln—for up to one year, after which the purified soul sits before God, or, in poetic terms, enters heaven. Children, and sometimes other relatives of the dead, recite the Kaddish ("Sanctification of God") prayer on behalf of their parents' souls in *Gehinnom*. Because it would be disrespectful to imply that one's parents need a whole year to be purified, the traditional Jewish period of mourning is eleven months. There is no need to mourn a soul basking in God's presence.

A famous rabbinic witticism comments on the idea that all souls go to the same place, regardless of how people live their earthly lives: The afterlife is like a giant synagogue, where prayer and study of Torah continue endlessly. To those who have trained properly in life, this is heaven. To others, it is hell.

WHAT DOES CHRISTIANITY TEACH ABOUT HEAVEN?

The key to the Christian understanding of heaven is contained in these words of Jesus: "I am the resurrection, and the life: he that believeth in me, though he were dead, yet shall he live. And whosoever liveth and believeth in me shall never die" (John 11:25–26).

Jesus, all of his disciples, and most of his early followers were Jews, so it is natural that Christian ideas of heaven and hell are built on Jewish foundations. However, these ideas were not necessarily accepted by all Jews or Christians. Jewish writers in the centuries preceding Jesus developed elaborate theologies of heaven and hell. But as Acts 23:8 notes, "The Sadducees say that there is no resurrection, neither angel, nor spirit: but the Pharisees confess both." The sect that wrote the Dead Sea Scrolls also believed in heaven and hell, and some scholars maintain that John the Baptist and perhaps also Jesus belonged to or studied with this group.

Nonetheless, the idea of resurrection was difficult to understand, as 1 Corinthians 15:12–19 makes clear. In this passage, Paul clarifies to church members in Corinth that they cannot consider themselves Christians if they deny resurrection:

> Now if Christ be preached that he rose from the dead, how say some among you that there is no resurrection of the dead? But if there be no resurrection of the dead, then is Christ not risen: And if Christ be not risen, then is our preaching in vain, and your faith is also vain. . . . For if the dead rise not, then is not Christ raised. And if Christ be not raised, your faith is vain; ye are yet in your sins. Then they also which are fallen asleep in Christ are perished. If in this life only we have hope in Christ, we are of all men most miserable.

This passage brings up another important Christian idea related to heaven: original sin. In the words of the *New England Primer*, the book that Puritan children used as their first reader, "In Adam's fall, we sinned all." That is, God's plan for humankind was eternal bliss. But by eating the forbidden fruit in the Garden of Eden, Adam and Eve brought sin and death into the world. All humans inherit this taint in their genetic makeup. To achieve salvation they must be purified of this original sin through Christ, the second Adam. As Paul says in 1 Corinthians 15:22, "For as in Adam all die, even so in Christ shall all be made alive." And as he elaborates in verses 42–47:

> So also is the resurrection of the dead. It is sown in corruption; it is raised in incorruption: It is sown in dishonour; it is raised in glory: it is sown in weakness; it is raised in power: It is sown a natural body; it is raised a spiritual body. . . . The first man Adam was made a living soul;

29

the last Adam was made a quickening spirit. . . . The first man is of the earth, earthy: the second man is the Lord from heaven.

The picture of heaven in the Gospels lacks concrete details. Jesus says in Matthew 5:12, "great is your reward in heaven," and in Mark 10:21, "thou shalt have treasure in heaven." Later Christian writings filled in the details. The Apocalypse of Peter, for example, speaks of angels carrying the righteous to a place with three fountains of wine, honey, and milk, where the earth brings forth fruit on its own, and where they will live a life without care.

Hell, on the other hand, is a place of "fierce fire" and "eternal gnashing of teeth," where the wicked "cry in torment" from hunger, thirst, and pain.

WHAT IS SPECIAL ABOUT CATHOLIC BELIEF?

In addition to heaven and hell, Catholic doctrine includes purgatory, a middle area in which certain souls are purged of their sins so that they can enter heaven.

In *Crossing the Threshold of Hope*, Pope John Paul II explains how studying the works of Saint John of the Cross helped him understand the concept of purgatory. Saint John speaks of a "living flame of love" and the pope sees this as a "purifying fire." According to this interpretation, Saint John's "dark night of the soul" is a type of purgatory. Because God is pure Love, He wants all humankind to share in His presence. But people hampered by the impurity of sin lack the ability to unite with God. Therefore, humans in this life can purge themselves of their physical nature, and souls in the next realm are given the chance to be purged of impurity in the fire of love. Far from being punishment, purgatory is a vehicle of God's love.

WHAT DOES İSLAM TEACH ABOUT HEAVEN?

Because it developed from many of the same sources, Islam naturally shares many ideas with Judaism and Christianity. Islam stresses the importance of submission to the One God, and the resulting reward for believers and punishment for infidels.

The Koran, the most sacred book of Islam, contains several graphic descriptions of heaven and hell. In heaven, rivers flow through beautiful gardens. Here the righteous will live forever, enjoying the most delicious fruits as well as the favors of beautiful maidens. In contrast, hell is a place of horrible fires fueled by the bodies of unbelievers. The wind in hell is burning hot, the waters boil, and the air is filled with the smoke of burning pitch. Souls in hell must eat bitter trees and drink boiling water.

These vivid pictures reflect the life of the desert dwellers who were the first followers of Islam. Heaven is like a wonderful oasis; hell is eternity in the howling desert wilderness. While some Muslims take these descriptions literally, many understand them as poetic images.

Perhaps the most famous expression in English of these Islamic ideas comes from *The Rubáiyát of Omar Khayyam*, by Edward FitzGerald:

A Book of Verses underneath the Bough,
A Jug of Wine, a Loaf of Bread—and Thou

31

Beside me singing in the Wilderness—
Oh, Wilderness were Paradise enow!

WHAT DOES THE BOOK OF MORMON SAY?

Here are some passages from the Book of Mormon that offer vivid descriptions of heaven and hell.

And being thus overcome with the Spirit, [Lehi] was carried away in a vision, even that he saw the heavens open, and he thought he saw God sitting upon his throne, surrounded with numberless concourses of angels in the attitude of singing and praising their God. And it came to pass that he saw one descending out of the midst of heaven, and he beheld that his lustre was above that of the sun at noon-day. And he also saw twelve others following him, and their brightness did exceed that of the stars in the firmament (1 Nephi 1:8–10).

The heaven is a place where God dwells and all his holy angels. . . . and he looketh down upon all the children of men; and he knows all the thoughts and intents of the heart; for by his hand were they all created from the beginning (Alma 18:30–33).

O my brethren, hearken unto my word; arouse the faculty of your soul; shake yourselves that ye may awake from the slumber of death; and loose yourselves from the pains of hell that ye may not become angels to the devil, to be cast into that lake of fire and brimstone which is the second death (Jacob 4:11).

O how great the goodness of our God, who prepareth a way for our escape from the grasp of this awful monster; yea, that monster death and hell, which I call the death of the body, and also the death of the spirit. And because of the way of deliverance of our God, the Holy One of Israel, this death, of which I have spoke, which is the temporal, shall deliver up its dead; which death is the grave. And this death of which I have spoken, which is the spiritual death, shall deliver up its dead; which spiritual death is hell; wherefore, death and hell must deliver up their dead, and hell must deliver up its captive spirits, and the grave must deliver up its captive bodies, and the bodies and the spirits of men will be restored one to the other; and it is by the power of the resurrection of the Holy One of Israel (2 Nephu 9:10–12).

WHAT IS SPECIAL ABOUT THE MORMON BELIEF IN HEAVEN?

Although they are Christians—members of the Church of Jesus Christ of Latter-Day Saints—Mormons have a number of beliefs that differ from those of other Christians.

According to Mormon belief, heaven is a place where families of the saints will be united and live together forever. Marriage lasts not only until death, but for all eternity. Unions that are not performed in a Mormon temple—for example, civil wedding ceremonies and marriages to a non-Mormon—will not continue in heaven. Spouses in such unions will be separated from each other and from their families in heaven, and they will spend eternity knowing what they have lost. This sense of loss is part of what might be called hell.

In addition, Mormons believe that even the dead can be baptized, through a proxy. As we have seen, being reunited with one's family is part of the reward of heaven. But because the Mormon Church was established in the nineteenth century, all Mormons have ancestors who were not members of the church. Therefore, it is very important to have a full record of one's family and to insure that all members are saved. For this reason, individual Mormons do extensive genealogical research, and the church maintains an archive with perhaps as many as two billion names! Ancestors who were not Mormons can be saved through a ceremony known as "baptism for the dead." As names of the dead are read aloud, a church member acting as a surrogate is baptized. Tens of millions of Mormons' ancestors have been baptized in this way.

In what church elders characterized as a misguided act of kindness, members of the Mormon faith performed proxy baptism for several hundred thousand Jewish victims of the Nazis, without the knowledge of surviving relatives. In 1991, and again in 1995, church leaders issued reminders that posthumous baptisms should be performed only for ancestors of living Mormons.

WHAT IS SPECIAL ABOUT THE BELIEF OF JEHOVAH'S WITNESSES?

Jehovah's Witnesses take Revelation 7:4 literally: "I heard the number of them which were sealed: and there were sealed a hundred and forty and four thousand of all the tribes of the children of Israel." They interpret this verse to mean that only a total of 144,000 people will enjoy the spiritual rewards of heaven. All others are fated to remain in the grave until they are resurrected to eternal life on earth.

Life on earth, however, is destined to change. With the coming of the new heaven and new earth, the reign of Satan will end. At that time political conflict will end, and there will be no more war or violence. In the words of Revelation 21:4: "God shall wipe away all tears from their eyes; and there shall be no more death, neither sorrow, nor crying, neither shall there be any more pain: for the former things are passed away."

According to this view, hell is not a place of eternal torment. It is merely the name of the place where those who do not go to heaven wait until the resurrection. In this sense, it might be equated with the grave.

WHAT DO CHRISTIAN SCIENTISTS BELIEVE ABOUT HEAVEN?

Christian Science teaches that heaven and hell are states of mind, not places. Christian Scientists believe that since God is all good, then He would not have created anything bad. Humankind is one of God's spiritual ideas and was not meant to suffer illness or death. These bad things can only be the result of errors of thought, and they exist only if people mistakenly allow them to exist. So too, heaven and hell. They exist in the mind of each person who, through thought and action, creates a personal heaven or hell in this life on earth.

WHAT DO SEVENTH-DAY ADVENTISTS SAY ABOUT HEAVEN AND HELL?

Adventists believe that the dead will be resurrected to eternal life after the second coming of Jesus Christ. Until then, the dead are asleep. The idea that the dead go right to heaven or hell, they say, is pagan mythology, and not supported by the Bible.

WHAT DO UNITARIAN UNIVERSALISTS BELIEVE ABOUT HEAVEN?

Unitarian Universalists do not interpret the Bible literally. They believe that the inspired message of the Bible is couched in the culture and experience of the human authors. Therefore, heaven and hell are metaphors for human states of mind. Heaven can be understood as love and compassion. Hell is injustice and violence. A Unitarian quoted in *Religions of America* said: "Our task is not to get men into Heaven; it is to get Heaven into men."

WHAT DOES BUDDHISM TEACH ABOUT HEAVEN?

According to Buddhism, humans can ascend through ever higher and more beautiful levels of paradise until they reach nirvana, the ultimate goal, which is a pure spiritual state beyond individual identity. Heaven, or paradise, is not forever and is not the ultimate goal of the virtuous. Through meditation and good deeds the soul can enjoy various levels of paradise, but it is always trying to travel higher, to unite with the supreme spirit. Some masters of spiritual enlightenment, known as *bodhisattvas*, are qualified to attain nirvana and become Buddhas. However, they choose to remain on earth to help others achieve their spiritual destiny. A *bodhisattva* accepts suffering without complaint, shows compassion to all living things, and strives to overcome human weaknesses such as pride, anger, and envy.

Souls that do not deserve paradise may suffer in hell, but not forever. The *bodhisattvas* have been known to enter hell in order to release favored students and other deserving souls.

WHAT DOES HINDUISM SAY ABOUT HEAVEN?

Hinduism teaches that an individual soul is reborn again and again in following generations. In each incarnation the soul must learn more about cosmic consciousness, or *atman*. One who has achieved great spirit (*maha atma*) is said to be a *mahatma*, as in the title given to Mohandas Gandhi, the great Indian spiritual and political leader.

WHAT ARE THE NATIVE AMERICAN BELIEFS ABOUT HEAVEN?

The beliefs of the Native Americans are captured in the well-known and somewhat condescending phrase, "Happy Hunting Ground." The Native Americans' original belief seems to have been that the spirits of the dead go to a place far away toward the end of the earth. There, they spend eternity hunting immortal animal spirits. In time, this spirit world was moved to the sky, perhaps because Native Americans were inspired by the flight of the eagle or the myth of the firebird.

With the coming of European settlers, many Native Americans adapted various aspects of Christianity into their beliefs. In 1799, the Seneca shaman Handsome Lake, who as a boy studied in a Quaker school, began expounding his *Kaiwiyoh*, or Good Message, which was a mixture of native beliefs and Quaker social behavior. In reply, the great chief Red Jacket and other prophets preached that if the tribes returned to their ancestral beliefs, the Europeans would disappear.

In 1870, after decades of war had almost destroyed the Native Americans, the Paiute developed the Ghost Dance religion. Although it quickly fell from view, it resurfaced again in 1888 through the preaching of a Paiute visionary named Wovoka. He taught a mystical system designed to prepare its followers for a reunion with their dead relatives and friends, as well as a spiritual transformation of the world. Because Wovoka identified himself as a type of messiah, and because he taught that Native American lands would be returned to them, white Americans feared that his movement would be violent, especially among the Sioux. It was suppressed by the army in several actions, including the famous massacre at Wounded Knee Creek in South Dakota.

CHAPTER THREE

WHAT DOES THE BIBLE SAY ABOUT HEAVEN?

HOW MANY TIMES IS HEAVEN MENTIONED IN THE BIBLE?

It is hard to give an exact number for several reasons. First, the content of the Bible differs among Jews, Protestants, and Catholics. The Jewish Bible—also called the Hebrew Bible—contains only what Protestants call the Old Testament. The Protestant Bible contains the Old and New Testaments, but omits a number of books—such as Tobit, Judith, Wisdom of Solomon, 1 and 2 Maccabees, and parts of Esther and other works—that Catholics consider part of the Old Testament. These books are included in some Protestant Bibles in a special section called *Apocrypha*.

Second, the Bible was composed in Hebrew, Aramaic, and Greek, and there are differences among English translations: one translation might say *heaven* where another says *sky*.

Third, it is unclear how many times to count mentions of

heaven in verses like Psalm 148:4, "Praise him, ye heavens of heavens and ye waters that be above the heavens."

We can say that Strong's *Exhaustive Concordance of the Bible* lists over seven hundred entries for heaven(s) in the King James Version, omitting the Apocrypha.

WHAT IS THE EARLIEST MENTION OF HEAVEN IN THE BIBLE?

The word *heaven* appears in the very first sentence of the Bible: "In the beginning God created the heaven and the earth."

In a sense the Bible also ends with heaven. Even though the word *heaven* itself does not appear in the last few sentences of Revelation, the final chapters are a description of the new heaven that will emerge at the end of time.

WHAT IS THE CONNECTION BETWEEN HEAVEN AND THE TOWER OF BABEL?

The Tower of Babel is the subject of the well-known story in Genesis 11 that explains the origin of the world's many languages. In the beginning, Adam and Eve and their family spoke one language: "And the whole earth was of one language, and of one speech." It came to pass, however, that as the population grew and settlements spread, and the people "journeyed from the east, that they found a plain in the land of Shinar, and they dwelt there." And in order to "make a name" for themselves, they decided, "Let us build us a city and a tower, whose top may reach unto heaven."

The tower was a symbol of excessive pride, an attempt to challenge the very heavens. Perhaps the people thought that such a tower would allow them to control the seasons or unseat God from His throne. In any case, God considered the building of the tower unacceptable: "And the Lord said, Behold, the people is one, and they have all one language; and this they begin to do: and now nothing will be restrained from them, which they have imagined to do."

God put a stop to the heaven-reaching tower by causing the builders to speak in different languages. Because they could no longer understand each other, the building stopped: "Go to, let us go down, and there confound their language, that they may not understand one another's speech. So the Lord scattered them abroad from thence upon the face of the earth: and they left off to build the city."

HOW MANY TIMES DOES JESUS MENTION HEAVEN?

In the King James translation, Jesus mentions heaven about 110 times. Here are some typical examples:

". . . the kingdom of heaven is at hand" (Matt. 4:17).

". . . your Father which is in heaven is perfect" (Matt. 5:48).

". . . it is given unto you to know the mysteries of the kingdom of heaven" (Matt. 13:11).

". . . sell whatsoever thou hast, and give to the poor, and thou shalt have treasure in heaven" (Mark 10:21).

". . . when they shall rise from the dead, they . . . are as the angels which are in heaven" (Mark 12:25).

"O Father, Lord of heaven and earth" (Luke 10:21).

". . . joy shall be in heaven over one sinner that repenteth, more than over ninety and nine just persons, which need no repentance" (Luke 15:7).

". . . no man hath ascended up to heaven, but he that came down from heaven, even the Son of man which is in heaven" (John 3:13).

"This is the bread which cometh down from heaven, that a man may eat thereof, and not die" (John 6:50).

In addition to the word *heaven*, Jesus uses the words *heavens* and *heavenly* a few times, as in Luke 11:13: ". . . how much more shall your heavenly Father give the Holy Spirit to them that ask him?"

WHAT WORDS DOES THE BIBLE USE FOR HEAVEN?

The King James Version of the Bible uses the word *heaven* to translate five Hebrew words, four Greek words, and one Aramaic word.

By far the most common Hebrew word rendered as *heaven* is *shamayim*. Among the hundreds of occurrences of *shamayim* are the following:

"In the beginning God created the heaven and the earth" (Gen. 1:1).

"I will rain bread from heaven for you" (Exod. 16:4).

"Look down from thy holy habitation, from heaven, and bless thy people Israel" (Deut. 26:15).

"Thus saith the Lord, The heaven is my throne, and the earth is my footstool" (Isa. 66:1).

The word *shakhaq* is translated as *heaven* twice in Psalm 89, verse 6: "For who in the heaven can be compared unto the Lord?" and in verse 37: "It shall be established for ever as the moon, and as a faithful witness in heaven."

In Psalm 77:18, the word *galgal* is rendered as *heaven*: "The voice of thy thunder was in the heaven."

In Psalm 68:4, the Hebrew word is *arabot*: ". . . extol him that rideth upon the heavens."

And in Isaiah 5:30, the Hebrew word is *ariyph*: ". . . the light is darkened in the heavens."

Aramaic, a close relative of Hebrew, is the language of parts of the book of Daniel. The word translated as *heaven* in these passages is *shemayah*, as in 2:28: ". . . there is a God in heaven that revealeth secrets."

The main word for *heaven* in the Greek of the New Testament is *ouranos*. Examples are:

"And lo a voice from heaven" (Matt. 3:17).

"And looking up to heaven, he sighed" (Mark 7:34).

". . . peace in heaven, and glory in the highest" (Luke 19:38).

"I saw the Spirit descending from heaven like a dove" (John 1:32).

In a number of places *heaven* translates compounds with *ouranos* or words built on this stem:

ouranothen in Acts 14:17: ". . . he did good, and gave us rain from heaven."

epouranios in Philippians 2:10: ". . . at the name of Jesus every knee should bow, of things in heaven, and things in earth, and things under the earth."

mesouranema in Revelation 8:13: "I beheld, and heard an angel flying through the midst of heaven. . . ."

We should also note that the word *heaven* is used differently in various translations of the Bible. For example, in the New International Version this last verse is rendered, "As I watched, I heard an eagle that was flying in midair. . . ." and in the New American Bible it is, "Then I looked again and heard an eagle flying high overhead. . . ."

IS HEAVEN A PLACE?

Most people think of heaven as a place. Certainly, if they are taken literally, many passages in the Bible imply that heaven is a place. For example:

"For this commandment which I command thee this day, it is not hidden from thee, neither is it far off. It is not in heaven, that thou shouldest say, Who shall go up for us to heaven, and bring it unto us, that we may hear it, and do it?" (Deut. 30:11–12).

"For ever, O Lord, thy word is settled in heaven" (Ps. 119:89).

"Lay not up for yourselves treasures upon earth, where moth and rust doth corrupt. . . . But lay up for yourselves treasures in heaven, where neither moth nor rust doth corrupt" (Matt. 6:19–20).

"And immediately I was in the spirit; and behold, a throne was set in heaven, and one sat on the throne" (Rev. 4:2).

IS HEAVEN THE SKY?

In many passages in the Bible, the word *heaven* seems to mean the sky. Quite a few examples bear this out:

"And God made the firmament, and divided the waters which were under the firmament from the waters which were above the firmament: . . . And God called the firmament heaven" (Gen. 1:7–8).

"And God made two great lights; the greater light to rule the day, and the lesser light to rule the night: he made the stars also. And God set them in the firmament of the heaven" (Gen. 1:16–17).

"Israel then shall dwell in safety alone: the fountain of Jacob shall be upon a land of corn and wine; also his heavens shall drop down dew" (Deut. 33:28).

"But in those days, after that tribulation, the sun shall be darkened, and the moon shall not give her light, And the stars of heaven shall fall. . . ." (Mark 13:24–25).

". . . he did good, and gave us rain from heaven, and fruitful seasons, filling our hearts with food and gladness" (Acts 14:17).

"And he prayed again, and the heaven gave rain, and the earth brought her fruit" (James 5:18).

It is common in English to use the word *heaven* when we mean sky. For example, it was said of Benjamin Franklin that "He snatched lightning from heaven, and the sceptre from tyrants."

In a famous speech in *The Merchant of Venice*, Shakespeare writes:

The quality of mercy is not strain'd,
It droppeth as the gentle rain from heaven
Upon the place beneath.

The English mystical poet William Blake says:
The moon like a flower
In heaven's high bower,
With silent delight
Sits and smiles on the night.

And the romantic poet Percy Bysshe Shelley speaks of:
Heaven's ebon vault,
Studded with stars unutterably bright,
Through which the moon's unclouded grandeur rolls.

IS HEAVEN IN OUTER SPACE?

Many passages in the Bible make it clear that heaven is above the earth. Genesis 49:25 speaks of "blessings of heaven above." In Deuteronomy 32:40, Moses says, "I lift up my hand to heaven." And Revelation 10:1 contains a vision of a "mighty angel come down from heaven, clothed with a cloud."

That heaven is very far above us is evident from Isaiah 55:9: "For as the heavens are higher than the earth, so are my ways higher than your ways, and my thoughts than your thoughts."

While ancient people may have imagined that heaven was right above the clouds, modern people know that airplanes do not fly to heaven. Accordingly, to some people's minds, heaven has been moved to outer space. In the early days of space travel, one Soviet cosmonaut told interviewers that he was convinced there is no God because he looked out the window of his spacecraft and did not see one. On the other hand, Carolyn Trickey-Bapty reports in *The Book of Angels* that cosmonauts on a later Soviet space flight claimed they saw seven giant, winged figures with halos in outer space.

IS HEAVEN THE HOME OF GOD?

The answer in the Bible is an unequivocal "Yes." The *Lord's Prayer* (Matt. 6:9ff, Luke 11:2ff) begins: "Our Father which art in heaven, Hallowed be thy name. Thy kingdom come.

Thy will be done in earth, as it is in heaven." And in numerous other places Jesus refers to "your Father which is in heaven" (e.g., Matt. 5:16, 6:1), "my Father which is in heaven" (e.g., Matt. 16:17), "your heavenly Father" (e.g., Luke 11:13, Matt. 6:14), and "my heavenly Father" (e.g., Matt. 15:13).

Here are some examples from the Hebrew Bible:

"And the Lord said, . . . Ye have seen that I have talked to you from heaven" (Exod. 20:22).

"Look down from thy holy habitation, from heaven, and bless thy people Israel" (Deut. 26:15).

"If I ascend up into heaven, thou art there" (Ps. 139:8).

"God is in heaven, and thou upon earth: therefore let thy words be few" (Eccles. 5:2).

Interestingly, the Israelites' teaching that God is in heaven was key to their understanding that He is universal. All other ancient people located gods in specific geographical places: There were sea gods, mountain gods, sun gods, gods of Canaan, gods of Egypt, gods of Athens. These were by definition gods who limited their concern to an assigned territory or people. But a God in heaven was a God of all creation and of all people. In the Bible, the One God who lives in heaven is concerned with the people of Babel (Gen. 11) and the people of Sodom and Gomorrah (Gen. 18–19), as well as the Egyptian handmaid Hagar (Gen. 16).

This idea of universality is captured in Robert Browning's famous line:

God's in his heaven—
All's right with the world.

On the other hand, King Solomon realized that God cannot be contained, even in the vastness of heaven. When he completed the temple in Jerusalem, Solomon expressed this understanding in a prayer (2 Chron. 6:18): "But will God in very deed dwell with men on earth? Behold, heaven and the heaven of heavens cannot contain thee; how much less this house which I have built!"

George Fox, the founder of the Society of Friends (Quakers), echoed this thought many centuries later: "The Lord showed me . . . that he did not dwell in these temples which men had commanded and set up, but in people's hearts."

IS HEAVEN ANOTHER NAME FOR GOD?

In poetic language there is a type of word-picture called metonymy, which uses a part to stand for the whole (for example, *hands* stands for *workers*), or an object to stand for a related idea (for example, *chair* substitutes for the person who chairs). In this way, the word *heaven* is often applied poetically to mean God, especially as a way to avoid taking the name of the Lord in vain. Hence, the origin of expressions like "Heaven help us" and "For heaven's sake."

In Luke 15:18, we find "I have sinned against heaven." And in Matthew 23:22, "And he that shall swear by heaven, sweareth by the throne of God, and by him that sitteth thereon."

Since supporters of monarchy often argued that kings were appointed by God's will, Shakespeare has King Lear say that when kings and nobles behave charitably to their subjects they "show the heavens more just." On a lighter note, Edgar Smith wrote early in the twentieth century that "Heaven will protect the Working Girl."

WHAT IS THE KINGDOM OF HEAVEN?

Because the word *heaven* can mean God, the phrase *Kingdom of Heaven* is another way of saying Kingdom of God, meaning that God is the King of all things. As Psalm 22:27–28 says:

> All the ends of the world shall remember and turn unto the Lord: and all the kindreds of the nations shall worship before thee. For the kingdom is the Lord's: and he is the governor among the nations.

And as Psalm 145:10–13 elaborates:
All thy works shall praise thee, O Lord; and thy saints shall bless thee.
They shall speak of the glory of thy kingdom, and talk of thy power;
To make known to the sons of men his mighty acts, and the glorious majesty of his kingdom.
Thy kingdom is an everlasting kingdom, and thy dominion endureth throughout all generations.

Some scholars understand the Kingdom of Heaven to mean the end of the world as we know it—the Day of the Lord mentioned by the Hebrew prophets (e.g., Zechariah 14). This connection finds support in 2 Peter 3:10: "the day of the Lord will come . . . in the which the heavens shall pass away." And it explains the preaching of Jesus that "the time is fulfilled, and the kingdom of God is at hand" (Mark 1:15), meaning that the end of time had arrived and the new age of God's kingship was to begin. Others believe that what Jesus meant by the Kingdom of Heaven is equivalent to what

51

people mean today by heaven. According to this view, the parables about the Kingdom of Heaven are descriptions of what people of any era must do to enter heaven.

WHAT ARE THE PEARLY GATES?

The Pearly Gates are the gates of heaven. According to the Book of Revelation (21:21), there are twelve gates in the new Jerusalem—the Holy City in heaven—and "every several gate was of one pearl." The phrase "pearly gates" was popularized by C. F. Taylor in 1853 in the hymn "The Roseate Hues":

Oh! for the pearly gates of heaven!
Oh! for the golden floor!

The gates of heaven are also called the Golden Gates, as in the hymn Henry Alford composed in 1866 and which was sung at his funeral five years later:

Ten thousand times ten thousand
In sparkling raiment bright,
The armies of the ransomed saints
Throng up the steps of light;
'Tis finished, all is finished,
Their fight with death and sin:
Fling open wide the golden gates,
And let the victors in.

What rush of aleluias
Fills all the earth and sky!
What ringing of a thousand harps
Bespeaks the triumph nigh!
O day, for which creation

And all the tribes were made;
O joy, for all its former woes
A thousand-fold repaid.

WHY DOES SAINT PETER SIT AT THE PEARLY GATES?

The popular imagination put Saint Peter at the Pearly Gates because Jesus made him the guardian of heaven, giving him the keys to the kingdom and the mandate to decide who may enter. Jesus says to Peter,

> Thou art Peter, and upon this rock I will build my church; and the gates of hell shall not prevail against it. And I will give unto thee the keys of the Kingdom of heaven: and whatsoever thou shalt bind on earth shall be bound in heaven: and whatsoever thou shalt loose on earth shall be loosed in heaven (Matt. 16:18–19).

Despite their reputation as joyless sourpusses, Puritans evidently had a sense of humor about religion. One tombstone from about 1630 reads:

A zealous Lock-Smith dyed of late,
And did arrive at heaven gate,
He stood without and would not knocke,
Because he meant to picke the locke.

An unluckier soul was the one who knocked politely on the Pearly Gates one night. When Saint Peter asked, "Who's there?" the soul responded, "It is I." Saint Peter replied, "Go to hell. We have enough English teachers here."

WHAT IS JACOB'S LADDER?

When Jacob fled from his brother Esau—fearing that Esau would kill him for stealing the blessing of the first born—he fell asleep at "a certain place."

> And he dreamed, and behold a ladder set up on the earth, and the top of it reached to heaven: and behold angels of God ascending and descending on it. And, behold, the Lord stood above it, and said, I am the Lord God of Abraham thy father, and the God of Isaac. . . . (Gen. 28:12–13).

Jacob's ladder became a symbol for the desire to climb to heaven. In the words of the old spiritual:

> We are climbing Jacob's ladder,
> We are climbing Jacob's ladder,
> We are climbing Jacob's ladder,
> Soldiers of the Cross.
>
> Every round goes higher, higher
> Every round goes higher, higher,
> Every round goes higher, higher,
> Soldiers of the Cross.
>
> We are climbing higher, higher,
> We are climbing higher, higher,
> We are climbing higher, higher,
> Soldiers of the Cross.

In modern usage, Jacob's ladder refers to the ladder hanging over the side of a boat; it is also a string design in the game cat's cradle.

WHERE IS THE GATE OF HEAVEN?

According to the Bible, the gate of heaven is located where Jacob's ladder stands. When Jacob awakens, he says, "Surely the Lord is in this place; and I knew it not. . . . How dreadful is this place! This is none other but the house of God, and this is the gate of heaven" (Gen. 28:16–17). Jacob then vows that if God preserves him and he is allowed to return home in peace, he will build God's house at this spot (vv. 21–22). For this reason, Jewish tradition equates the "certain place" (v. 11) with the Temple Mount in Jerusalem.

Incidentally, Tien An Men Square in Beijing (often spelled incorrectly as one word, *Tienanmen*) means literally "Heavenly Peace Gate" Square.

CHAPTER FOUR

WHAT ARE SOME MEMORABLE PASSAGES IN THE BIBLE ABOUT HEAVEN?

HERE ARE A FEW:

"In the beginning God created the heaven and the earth" (Gen. 1:1).

"And God said, Let there be a firmament in the midst of the waters, and let it divide the waters from the waters" (Gen. 1:6).

"And God called the firmament heaven" (Gen. 1:8).

"And God said, Let there be lights in the firmament of the heaven to divide the day from the night" (Gen. 1:14).

". . . the same day were all the fountains of the great deep broken up, and the windows of heaven were opened" (Gen. 7:11).

". . . let us build a city and a tower, whose top may reach unto heaven" (Gen. 11:4).

"Blessed be Abram of the most high God, possessor of heaven and earth" (Gen. 14:19).

"Then the Lord rained upon Sodom and Gomorrah brimstone and fire from the Lord out of heaven" (Gen. 19:24).

"I will multiply thy seed as the stars of the heaven" (Gen. 22:17).

"How dreadful is this place! this is none other but the house of God, and this is the gate of heaven" (Gen. 28:17).

"Behold, I will rain bread from heaven for you" (Exod. 16:4).

"Ye have seen that I have talked with you from heaven" (Exod. 20:22).

"I call heaven and earth to witness against you this day" (Deut. 4:26).

"Behold, the heaven and the heaven of heavens is the Lord's thy God, the earth also, with all that therein is" (Deut. 10:14).

"That your days may be multiplied, and the days of your children . . . as the days of heaven upon the earth" (Deut. 11:21).

"Look down from thy holy habitation, from heaven, and bless thy people Israel" (Deut. 26:15).

"There is none like unto the God of Jeshurun, who rideth upon the heaven in thy help, and in his excellency on the sky" (Deut. 33:26).

"So the sun stood still in the midst of heaven" (Josh. 10:13).

"And Absalom rode upon a mule . . . and his head caught hold of the oak, and he was taken up between the heaven and the earth" (2 Sam. 18:9).

"Then the earth shook and trembled; the foundations of heaven moved and shook" (2 Sam. 22:8).

"Then hear thou in heaven, and forgive the sin of thy people Israel" (1 Kings 8:34).

"Elijah went up by a whirlwind into heaven" (2 Kings 2:11).

"But who is able to build him a house, seeing the heaven and heaven of heavens cannot contain him?" (2 Chron. 2:6).

"We are the servants of the God of heaven and earth" (Ezra 5:11).

"It is as high as heaven; what canst thou do? deeper than hell; what canst thou know?" (Job 11:8).

"The heaven shall reveal his iniquity" (Job 20:27).

"Knowest thou the ordinances of heaven?" (Job 38:33).

"The Lord is in his holy temple, the Lord's throne is in heaven" (Ps. 11:4).

"Let the heaven and earth praise him, the seas, and every thing that moveth therein" (Ps. 69:34).

"Thou didst cause judgment to be heard from heaven" (Ps. 76:8).

"Truth shall spring out of the earth; and righteousness shall look down from heaven" (Ps. 85:11).

"For as the heaven is high above the earth, so great is his mercy toward them that fear him" (Ps. 103:11).

"If I ascend up into heaven, thou art there; if I make my bed in hell, behold, thou art there" (Ps. 139:8).

"To every thing there is a season, and a time to every purpose under the heaven" (Eccles. 3:1).

"God is in heaven, and thou upon the earth: therefore let thy words be few" (Eccles. 5:2).

"I saw also the Lord sitting upon a throne, high and lifted up, and his train filled the temple. Above it stood the seraphim . . . . And one cried unto another, and said, Holy, holy, holy, is the Lord of hosts" (Isa. 6:1–3).

"How art thou fallen from heaven, O Lucifer, son of the morning!" (Isa. 14:12).

"And all the host of heaven shall be dissolved, and the heavens shall be rolled together as a scroll" (Isa. 34:4).

"O Lord of hosts, God of Israel, that dwellest between the cherubims, thou art the God, even thou alone, of all the kingdoms of the earth: thou hast made heaven and earth" (Isa. 37:16).

"Who hath measured the waters in the hollow of his hand, and meted out heaven with the span? . . ." (Isa. 40:12).

"Thus saith the Lord, The heaven is my throne, and the earth is my footstool" (Isa. 66:1).

". . . be not dismayed at the signs of heaven" (Jer. 10:2).

"He hath made the earth by his power, he hath established the world by his wisdom, and hath stretched out the heaven by his understanding" (Jer. 51:15).

"And above the firmament that was over their heads was the likeness of a throne, as the appearance of a sapphire stone: and upon the likeness of the throne was the likeness as the appearance of a man" (Ezek. 1:26).

"Then the spirit took me up, and I heard behind me a voice of a great rushing, saying, Blessed be the glory of the Lord from his place" (Ezek. 3:12).

". . . the king saw a watcher and a holy one coming down from heaven" (Dan. 4:23).

". . . praise and extol and honor the King of heaven, all whose works are truth, and his ways judgment" (Dan. 4:37).

". . . he worketh signs and wonders in heaven and in earth" (Dan. 6:27).

". . . behold, one like the Son of man came with the clouds of heaven" (Dan. 7:13).

"Though they dig into hell, thence shall mine hand take them; though they climb up to heaven, thence will I bring them down" (Amos 9:2).

"Repent ye: for the kingdom of heaven is at hand" (Matt. 3:2).

"Blessed are the poor in spirit: for theirs is the kingdom of heaven" (Matt. 5:3).

"Rejoice, and be exceeding glad: for great is your reward in heaven" (Matt. 5:12).

"Till heaven and earth pass, one jot or one tittle shall in no wise pass from the law, till all be fulfilled" (Matt. 5:18).

"Be ye therefore perfect, even as your Father which is in heaven is perfect" (Matt. 5:48).

"Our Father which art in heaven, Hallowed be thy name. Thy kingdom come. Thy will be done in earth, as it is in heaven" (Matt. 6:9–10).

". . . lay up for yourselves treasures in heaven" (Matt. 6:20).

". . . it is given unto you to know the mysteries of the kingdom of heaven" (Matt. 13:11).

"The kingdom of heaven is like to a grain of mustard seed" (Matt. 13:31).

"I will give unto thee the keys of the kingdom of heaven: and whatsoever thou shalt bind on earth shall be bound in heaven: and whatsoever thou shalt loose on earth shall be loosed in heaven" (Matt. 16:19).

"Except ye be converted, and become as little children, ye shall not enter into the kingdom of heaven" (Matt. 18:3).

"Suffer little children . . . to come unto me: for of such is the kingdom of heaven" (Matt. 19:14).

". . . go and sell that thou hast, and give to the poor, and thou shalt have treasure in heaven" (Matt. 19:21).

"Immediately after the tribulation of those days shall the sun be darkened, and the moon shall not give her light, and the stars shall fall from heaven, and the powers of the heavens shall be shaken: And then shall appear the sign of the Son of man in heaven: and then shall all the tribes of the earth mourn, and they shall see the Son of man coming in the clouds of heaven with power and great glory" (Matt. 24:29–30).

"And there came a voice from heaven, saying, Thou art my beloved Son, in whom I am well pleased" (Mark 1:11).

". . . he shall receive . . . in the world to come eternal life" (Mark 10:30).

"For when they shall rise from the dead, they neither

marry, nor are given in marriage; but are as the angels which are in heaven" (Mark 12:25).

". . . ye shall see the Son of man sitting on the right hand of power, and coming in the clouds of heaven" (Mark 14:62).

"I beheld Satan as lightning fall from heaven" (Luke 10:18).

". . . rejoice, because your names are written in heaven" (Luke 10:20).

". . . thou shalt be recompensed at the resurrection of the just" (Luke 14:14).

". . . joy shall be in heaven over one sinner that repenteth, more than over ninety and nine just persons, which need no repentance" (Luke 15:7).

"Blessed be the King that cometh in the name of the Lord: peace in heaven, and glory in the highest" (Luke 19:38).

"I saw the Spirit descending from heaven like a dove" (John 1:32).

". . . no man hath ascended up to heaven, but he that came down from heaven, even the Son of man which is in heaven" (John 3:13).

". . . whosoever believeth in him should not perish, but have eternal life" (John 3:15).

"A man can receive nothing, except it be given him from heaven" (John 3:27).

"Moses gave you not that bread from heaven; but my Father giveth you the true bread from heaven. For the bread of God is he which cometh down from heaven, and giveth life unto the world" (John 6:32–33).

"And suddenly there came a sound from heaven as of a rushing mighty wind" (Acts 2:2).

"And as he journeyed, he came near Damascus: and suddenly there shined round about him a light from heaven" (Acts 9:3).

"For the wrath of God is revealed from heaven against all ungodliness and unrighteousness of men, who hold the truth in unrighteousness" (Rom. 1:18).

"The first man is of the earth, earthy: the second man is the Lord from heaven" (1 Cor. 15:47).

". . . the hope which is laid up for you in heaven" (Col. 1:5).

"Masters, give unto your servants that which is just and equal; knowing that ye also have a Master in heaven" (Col. 4:1).

"For the Lord himself shall descend from heaven with a shout, with the voice of the archangel, and with the trump of God" (1 Thess. 4:16).

"We have such a high priest, who is set on the right hand of the throne of the Majesty in the heavens" (Heb. 8:1).

"But the day of the Lord will come as a thief in the night; in the which the heavens shall pass away with a great noise" (2 Pet. 3:10).

". . . new Jerusalem, which cometh down out of heaven from my God" (Rev. 3:12).

". . . behold, a door was opened in heaven: and the first voice which I heard was as it were of a trumpet talking with me; which said, Come up hither, and I will shew thee things which must be hereafter. And immediately I was in the spirit; and, behold, a throne was set in heaven, and one sat on the throne" (Rev. 4:1–2).

"And there was war in heaven: Michael and his angels fought against the dragon; and the dragon fought and his angels" (Rev. 12:7).

". . . rejoice, ye heavens, and ye that dwell in them" (Rev. 12:12).

"And I heard a voice from heaven, as the voice of many waters, and as the voice of a great thunder: and I heard the voice of harpers harping with harps" (Rev. 14:2).

"And after these things I heard a great voice of much people in heaven, saying, Alleluia; Salvation, and glory, and honor, and power, unto the Lord our God" (Rev. 19:1).

"And I saw an angel come down from heaven, having the

key of the bottomless pit and a great chain in his hand" (Rev. 20:1).

"And I saw a new heaven and a new earth: for the first heaven and the first earth were passed away" (Rev. 21:1).

CHAPTER FIVE

WHAT ARE THE PARABLES OF THE KINGDOM OF HEAVEN?

In Matthew 13, 18, 20, 22, and 25, Jesus explains the nature of God's kingdom in a series of parables. They are:

THE SOWER (13:3–8)

Behold, a sower went forth to sow; And when he sowed, some seeds fell by the way side, and the fowls came and devoured them up: Some fell upon stony places, where they had not much earth: and forthwith they sprung up, because they had no deepness of earth: And when the sun was up, they were scorched; and because they had no root, they withered away. And some fell among thorns; and the thorns sprung up, and choked them: But other fell into good ground, and brought forth fruit, some a hundredfold, some sixtyfold, some thirtyfold.

THE GOOD AND BAD SEED (13:24–30)

The kingdom of heaven is likened unto a man which sowed good seed in his field. But while men slept, his enemy came and sowed tares among the wheat, and went his way. But when the blade was sprung up, and brought forth fruit, then appeared the tares also. So the servants of the householder came and said unto him . . . Wilt thou then that we go and gather them up? But he said, Nay; lest while ye gather up the tares, ye root up also the wheat with them. Let both grow together until the harvest: and in the time of the harvest I will say to the reapers, Gather ye together first the tares, and bind them in bundles to burn them: but gather the wheat into my barn.

THE MUSTARD SEED (13:31–32)

The kingdom of heaven is like to a grain of mustard seed, which a man took, and sowed in his field: Which indeed is the least of all seeds: but when it is grown, it is the greatest among herbs, and becometh a tree, so that the birds of the air come and lodge in the branches thereof.

YEAST (13:33)

The kingdom of heaven is like unto leaven, which a woman took, and hid in three measures of meal, till the whole was leavened.

BURIED TREASURE (13:44)

Again, the kingdom of heaven is like unto treasure hid in a field; the which when a man hath found, he hideth, and for joy thereof goeth and selleth all that he hath, and buyeth that field.

THE PEARL (13:45–46)

Again, the kingdom of heaven is like unto a merchant man, seeking goodly pearls: Who, when he had found one pearl of great price, went and sold all that he had, and bought it.

THE NET CAST INTO THE SEA (13:47–48)

Again, the kingdom of heaven is like unto a net, that was cast into the sea, and gathered of every kind: Which, when it was full, they drew to shore, and sat down, and gathered the good into vessels, but cast the bad away.

THE DEBTOR (18:23–34)

Therefore is the kingdom of heaven likened unto a certain king, which would take account of his servants. And when he had begun to reckon, one was brought unto him, which owed him ten thousand talents. But forasmuch as he had not to pay, his lord commanded him to be sold, and his wife, and children, and all that he had, and payment to be made. The servant therefore fell down, and worshipped him, saying, Lord, have patience with me, and I will pay thee all. Then the lord of that servant was moved with compassion, and loosed him, and forgave him the debt. But the same servant went out, and found one of his fellow-servants, which owed him a hundred pence: and he laid hands on him, and took him by the throat, saying, Pay me that thou owest . . . and cast him into prison, till he should pay the debt. So when his fellow-servants saw what was done, they were very sorry, and came and told unto their lord all that was done. Then his lord . . . said unto him, O thou wicked servant, I forgave thee all that debt, because thou desiredst me: Shouldest not thou also have had compassion on thy fellow-servant, even as I had pity on thee? And his lord was wroth, and delivered him to the tormentors, till he should pay all that was due unto him.

THE LABORERS IN THE VINEYARD (20:1–15)

For the kingdom of heaven is like unto a man . . . which went out early in the morning to hire laborers into his vineyard. And when he had agreed with the laborers for a penny a day, he sent them into his vineyard. And he went out about the third hour, and saw others standing idle in the market-place, And said unto them; Go ye also into the vineyard, and whatsoever is right I will give you. And they went their way. Again he went out about the sixth and ninth hour, and did likewise. And about the eleventh hour he went out, and found others standing idle. . . . He saith unto them, Go ye also into the vineyard; and whatsoever is right, that shall ye receive. So when even was come, the lord of the vineyard saith to his stew-ard, Call the laborers. . . . And when they came that were hired about the eleventh hour, they received every man a penny. But when the first came, they supposed that they should have received more; and they likewise received every man a penny. And when they received it, they murmured against the good-man of the house, Saying, These last have wrought but one hour, and thou hast made them equal unto us, which have borne the burden and heat of the day. But he answered . . . Friend, I do thee no wrong: didst not thou agree with me for a penny? Take that thine is, and go thy way: I will give unto this last, even as unto thee. Is it not lawful for me to do what I will with mine own? Is thine eye evil, because I am good?

THE MARRIAGE OF THE KING'S SON (22:2–14)

The kingdom of heaven is like unto a certain king, which made a marriage for his son, And sent forth his servants to call them that were bidden to the wedding: and they would not come. Again, he sent forth other servants, saying, Tell them which are bidden, Behold, I have prepared my dinner: my oxen and my fatlings are killed, and all things are ready: come unto the marriage. But they made light of it, and went their ways, one to his farm, another to his merchandise: And the remnant took his servants, and entreated them spitefully, and slew them. But when the king heard thereof, he was wroth: and he sent forth his armies, and destroyed those murderers, and burned up their city. Then saith he to his servants, The wedding is ready, but they which were bidden were not worthy. Go ye therefore into the highways, and as many as ye shall find, bid to the marriage. So those servants . . . gathered together all as many as they found, both bad and good . . . And when the king came in to see the guests, he saw there a man which had not on a wedding garment. . . . Then said the king to the servants, Bind him hand and foot, and take him away, and cast him into outer darkness; there shall be weeping and gnashing of teeth. For many are called, but few are chosen.

THE TEN VIRGINS (25:1–12)

Then shall the kingdom of heaven be likened unto ten virgins, which took their lamps, and went forth to meet the bridegroom. And five of them were wise, and five were foolish. They that were foolish took their lamps, and took no oil with them: But the wise took oil in their vessels with their lamps. While the bridegroom tarried, they all slumbered and slept. And at midnight there was a cry made, Behold, the bridegroom cometh; go ye out to meet him. Then all those virgins arose, and trimmed their lamps. And the foolish said unto the wise, Give us of your oil; for our lamps are gone out. But the wise answered, saying, Not so; lest there be not enough for us and you: but go ye rather to them that sell, and buy for yourselves. And while they went to buy, the bridegroom came; and they that were ready went in with him to the marriage: and the door was shut. Afterward came also the other virgins, saying, Lord, Lord, open to us. But he answered and said, Verily I say unto you, I know you not.

THE TALENTS (Matthew 25:14–30)

For the kingdom of heaven is as a man travelling into a far country, who called his own servants, and delivered unto them his goods. And unto one he gave five talents, to another two, and to another one; to every man according to his several ability; . . . Then he that had received the five talents went and traded with the same, and made them other five talents. And likewise he that had received two, he also gained other two. But he that had received one went and digged in the earth, and hid his lord's money. After a long time the lord of those servants cometh, and reckoneth with them. And so he that had received five talents came and brought other five talents . . . . His lord said unto him, Well done, thou good and faithful servant . . . . He also that had received two talents came . . . . His lord said unto him, Well done, good and faithful servant . . . . Then he which had received the one talent came . . . . His lord answered and said unto him, Thou wicked and slothful servant . . . Thou oughtest therefore to have put my money to the exchangers, and then at my coming I should have received mine own with usury . . . .

CHAPTER SIX

WHAT DO FAMOUS AMERICANS THINK ABOUT HEAVEN AND HELL?

President BILL CLINTON, speaking at a memorial service for those killed in the 1995 Oklahoma City bombing:

Those who are lost now belong to God. Some day we will be with them. But until that happens, their legacy must be our lives.

BILLY GRAHAM, evangelist:

As God, our loving Father, looks on, we, His disobedient children, continue to disobey. It would not be just for Him to let our sins go unpunished. Justice requires judgment. But God loves us. . . There is a final judgment coming, but God hates that day and continues to postpone it that the world might be saved.

Approaching Hoofbeats

MARK TWAIN, nineteenth-century humorist:

In man's heaven everybody sings! . . . This universal singing is not casual, not occasional, not relieved by intervals of quiet; it goes on, all day long, and every day, during a stretch of twelve hours. And everybody stays; whereas in the earth the place would be empty in two hours.

Letters from the Earth

PHILLIS WHEATLEY, eighteenth-century slave and poet:

'Twas mercy brought me from my Pagan land,
Taught my benighted soul to understand
That there's a God, that there's a Saviour too:
Once I redemption neither sought nor knew.
Some view our sable race with scornful eye,
"Their colour is a diabolic die."
Remember, Christians, Negroes, black as Cain,
May be refin'd, and join th' angelic train.

"On Being Brought from Africa to America"

BENJAMIN FRANKLIN, inventor and founding father:

During his lifetime, Franklin was respected throughout the western world as a scientist; he was especially revered by both the Americans and the French. The inscription beneath one bust of Franklin reads:

Eripuit coelo fulmen, sceptrumque tyrannis.

(He snatched lightning from heaven, and the scepter from tyrants.)

The epitaph that he composed for himself is more light-hearted, but certainly as sincere:

The body of
Benjamin Franklin, printer,
(Like the cover of an old book,
Its contents worn out,
And stript of its lettering and gilding)

72

Lies here, food for worms!
Yet the work itself shall not be lost,
For it will, as he believed, appear once more
In a new
And more beautiful edition,
Corrected and amended
By its Author!

THOMAS JEFFERSON, third president of the United States:
An eloquent preacher . . . [said] he did not believe there
was a Quaker, Presbyterian, Methodist, or Baptist in heaven.
Having paused to give his hearers time to stare and wonder, he
added that in heaven God knew no distinctions but considered all good men his children. . . . [H]e who steadily observes
those moral precepts in which all religions concur will never
be questioned at the gates of heaven as to the dogmas in which
they all differ.

THOMAS PAINE, revolutionary:
As several of my colleagues . . . have given me the example
of making their voluntary and individual profession of faith, I
also will make mine: . . .
I believe in one God, and no more; and hope for happiness
beyond this life.
I believe in the equality of man, and I believe that religious
duties consist in doing justice, loving mercy, and endeavoring
to make our fellow-creatures happy.
The Age of Reason

Despite this profession of faith, Paine was widely regarded
as a heretic because of his attacks on Christianity in *The Age
of Reason* and because he supported antichurch activities during
the French Revolution. He even figures, along with the devil,
in a hymn written in about 1807:

73

The world, the Devil, and Tom Paine,
Have tried their force, but all in vain;
They can't prevail, the reason is
The Lord defends the Methodist.

They pray, they sing, they preach the best,
And do the Devil most molest;
If Satan had his vicious way,
He'd kill and damn them all today.

They are despised by Satan's train,
Because they shout and preach so plain;
I'm bound to march in endless bliss,
And die a shouting Methodist.

AMBROSE BIERCE, nineteenth-century satirist:
Heaven. A place where the wicked cease from troubling
you with talk of their personal affairs, and the good listen with
attention while you expound your own.
The Devil's Dictionary

WALT WHITMAN, nineteenth-century poet:
I do not know what follows the death of my body,
But I know well that whatever it is, it is best for me,
And I know well that whatever is really me shall live
just as much as before.
Leaves of Grass

WILLIAM TECUMSEH SHERMAN, Civil War general:
War is Hell.

EMILY DICKINSON, nineteenth-century poet:
Some keep the Sabbath going to Church—
I keep it, staying at home . . . .

God preaches, a noted Clergyman—
And the sermon is never long,
So instead of getting to Heaven, at last—
I'm going, all along.

WILLIAM JAMES, nineteenth-century philosopher:
The hell to be endured hereafter, of which theology tells, is
no worse than the hell we make for ourselves in this world by
habitually fashioning our characters in the wrong way.
The Principles of Psychology

BABE RUTH, baseball legend:
In an essay that he wrote in 1948 for *Guideposts* magazine,
Babe Ruth recalled his troubled youth and the religious teachers who helped him find his way. Here he describes his turn-
ing point:
As I look back now, I realize that knowledge of God was a
big crossroads with me. I got one thing straight (and I wish all
kids did)—that God was Boss. He was not only my Boss but
Boss of all my bosses. . . . I also realized that God was not only
just, but merciful. He knew we were weak and that we all
found it easier to be stinkers than good sons of God. . . .
Ruth's work with young people was widely publicized.
When he died, he was honored with this inscription by New
York's Cardinal Spellman for his tombstone in Gate of Heaven
cemetery:
May the Divine Spirit that animated Babe Ruth to win the
crucial game of life inspire the youth of America.

ANNE BRADSTREET, colonial New England poet:
So he that failest in this world of pleasure,
Feeding on sweets, that never bit of th' sour,
That's full of friends, of honor, and of treasure,
Fond fool, he takes this earth ev'n for heaven's bower.

But sad affliction comes and makes him see
Here's neither honor, wealth, nor safety;
Only above is found all with security.
Contemplations

CHAPTER SEVEN

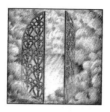

WHAT DO RELIGIOUS THINKERS SAY ABOUT HEAVEN AND HELL?

PLATO

Although the Greek philosopher Plato lived in Athens some four centuries before Jesus, his ideas influenced many Christian theologians, including Origen, Augustine, and Anselm. Plato believed that "universal ideas" exist in a spiritual realm—a place we might think of as the mind of God. Physical objects like trees, tools, animals, or humans are judged according to how closely they approach the universal ideal of a tree, tool, animal, or human.

He also taught that human knowledge, derived as it is from observation or logic, can never be total because of the limitations of all human experience. True knowledge exists only in the spiritual realm, where the soul has access to it. In contrast to opinions based on experience, true knowledge comes only when the soul remembers what it has learned from God. The goal of human life, according to Plato, is to achieve this true knowledge of the Good. Knowledge leads to virtue—people who know what is right will do what is right—and virtue leads to happiness.

AUGUSTINE

In *The City of God*, Augustine, the early Christian Church Father and author, compares the earthly world to the heavenly city. Life on earth, he says, is full of sin and suffering. But in the afterlife, according to Augustine, we shall enjoy ". . . all that God the creator of all natures has bestowed upon ours." These gifts from God are not only good, but eternal. They are not only of the spirit, but of the body, which will be revitalized by the resurrection. In this place of peace and security, "the virtues shall no longer be struggling against any vice or evil, but shall enjoy the reward of victory, the eternal peace which no adversary shall disturb."

MOSES MAIMONIDES, twelfth-century Jewish philosopher:

Maimonides remains the greatest Jewish philosopher and one of the intellectual giants of all time. His work, especially his attempt to harmonize Aristotle and Judaism, influenced Thomas Aquinas and many other Christian thinkers.

The Hebrew Bible—the Torah—stresses ethical behavior; Judaism does not have a confession of faith similar to the Apostle's Creed or the Nicene Creed of Christianity. Maimonides, however, composed his own personal "Thirteen Principles of Faith." He begins with: "I firmly believe that the Creator, blessed be his name, is the creator and ruler of all created things. . . ." His final principle is: "I firmly believe that there will be a revival of the dead when it pleases the Creator, and his name will be exalted forever." Maimonides' principles are accepted by many Jews and have been incorporated into the traditional prayerbook.

THOMAS AQUINAS, thirteenth-century Christian philosopher and theologian:

Aquinas's great work is the monumental *Summa Theologica*, a systematic presentation of Christian doctrine presented in a kind of "question and answer" format. Aquinas poses the question of how souls, which have no material substance, can enjoy reward or suffer pain. He answers that souls can be assigned "places" in a figurative sense, as though they were real, material beings. Each soul's place is determined by its nature, as each human (in Aquinas's medieval world) is assigned a place in society according to his or her nature. Souls receive their assigned place "according as they more or less approach to the first substance . . . namely God"—who naturally has the highest place. The result? "Those souls that have a perfect share in the Godhead are in heaven, and those souls that are deprived of that share are assigned to a contrary place," perhaps a place we might think of as hell.

SIR THOMAS BROWNE, seventeenth-century English physician and mystic:

In his confession of faith, *Religio Medici* (The Religion of a Doctor), Browne wrote:

"The heart of man is the place the devils dwell in: I feel sometimes a hell within myself."

JONATHAN EDWARDS, colonial New England minister:

. . . men are held in the hand of God, over the pit of hell; they have deserved the fiery pit, and are already sentenced to it; and God is dreadfully provoked . . . and they have done nothing in the least to appease or abate that anger, neither is God in the least bound by any promise to hold them up one moment; the devil is waiting for them, hell is gaping for them, the flames gather and flash about them, and would fain lay hold of them, and swallow them up.

"Sinners in the Hands of an Angry God"

WILLIAM BLAKE, eighteenth-century English mystic and poet:

Mutual Forgiveness of each vice,
Such are the Gates of Paradise.
The Gates of Paradise

He who shall teach the child to doubt,
The rotting grave shall ne'er get out.
Auguries of Innocence

JOSEPH SMITH, Mormon prophet:

In his account of the vision he had on September 21, 1823, Smith described the angel Moroni, who told him where to find the golden plates containing the Book of Mormon:

> . . . I discovered a light appearing in my room, which continued to increase until the room was lighter than at noonday, when immediately a personage appeared at my bedside, standing in the air, for his feet did not touch the floor. He had on a loose robe of most exquisite whiteness. It was a whiteness beyond anything earthly I had ever seen . . . . Not only was his robe white, but his whole person was glorious beyond description, and his countenance truly like lightning. The room was exceeding light, but not so very bright as immediately around his person. . . .
>
> After this communication, I saw the light in the room begin to gather immediately around the person of him who had been speaking to me, and it continued to do so, until the room was again left dark, except just around him, when instantly I saw, as it were, a conduit open right up to heaven, and he ascended until he entirely disappeared, and the room was left as it had been before this heavenly light had made its appearance.

MARY BAKER EDDY, founder of Christian Science:

The sinner makes his own hell by doing evil, the saint his own heaven by doing right.

JOHN HENRY, Cardinal Newman:

Weep not for me:
Be blithe as wont, nor tinge with gloom
The stream of love that circles home,
Light hearts and free!
Joy in the gifts Heaven's bounty lends,
Nor miss my face, dear friends!
I still am near.
A Voice from Afar

ALBERT SCHWEITZER, French philosopher and Nobel Peace
Prize winner:

An interesting question about the Resurrection of the Dead
is: What happens at the end of time to people who have not
died? Do they somehow share in the Resurrection? In *The Last
Supper,* Schweitzer answers that the Resurrection will affect
everyone: it will raise existence on earth to a higher plane. Those
who have already died will have to be brought back to life. But
even those who are alive will experience a transformation. The
Resurrection is the first stage of the messianic era. And it does
not matter whether we enter the Kingdom of God from life or
death. Compared to the Kingdom, everything is death.

POPE JOHN PAUL II:

In *Crossing the Threshold of Hope,* Pope John Paul II explains
why religion offers a kind of hope that science cannot. Science
has given us better health and longer life. But it cannot free us
from death—the ultimate human evil. Only religion can do
that. For, says the Pope, "Death itself is no longer that kind of
evil, if followed by the Resurrection. . . . And what is this eternal life? It is happiness that comes from union with God."

CHAPTER EIGHT

WHAT IS HEAVEN LIKE?

WHAT IS THE DOME OF HEAVEN?

Ancient people believed that the sky or heaven was like an upside-down bowl over the earth, touching the earth at the horizon and soaring overhead in the center. The sun, moon, and stars were thought to be lodged in this dome. Some people believed that the bowl rested on four pillars, as we see in Job 26:11: "The pillars of heaven tremble." We can perhaps picture this "dome of heaven" more easily if we think of the dome of a mosque.

WHAT ARE THE WINDOWS OF HEAVEN?

Given the belief that heaven was solid, like a dome, it was thought that there were windows (and perhaps doors) to allow entry and exit for angels, souls, and rain. In Genesis 7:11, the flood in the days of Noah is described as beginning when "all the fountains of the great deep [were] broken up, and the windows of heaven were opened."

There is yet another reference to "windows of heaven" in 2 Kings 7:2. An opponent of the prophet Elisha doubts his prophecy that a miracle will end the famine in Samaria overnight and cause the price of food to drop sharply. The opponent taunts the prophet by saying, "Behold, if the Lord would make windows in the heaven, might this thing be?"

WHAT IS THE WEATHER LIKE IN HEAVEN?

Since heaven is a place of perfect pleasure, it follows that the weather there is always perfect. Of course, this means different things to different people. To the desert-dwelling Arabs, heaven is a shady oasis with cool, gentle breezes. To the Greeks, the Elysian fields were always temperate, without snow or storm.

WHAT DOES HEAVEN LOOK LIKE?

According to the Koran, heaven is full of spreading shade trees and thornless trees laden with fruit. Rivers flow through luxurious gardens. This description is very similar to the one in the Book of the Secrets of Enoch, which talks of sweet-flowered trees bearing fragrant fruit, and two springs flowing with milk and honey.

Revelation 21 pictures heaven as a beautiful city, with pearl gates and streets of gold. Milton alludes to this vision in *Paradise Lost*, when he says that the angel Mammon lusted after the riches of heaven even before his fall from grace:

> . . . even in heaven his looks and thoughts
> Were always downward bent, admiring more
> The riches of heaven's pavement, trodden gold,
> Than aught divine. . . .

ARE THERE PLANTS IN HEAVEN?

Many people imagine heaven as a beautiful garden. The following hymn, which was very popular in seventeenth-century Scotland, speaks of the heavenly city of Jerusalem as a place laden with greenery:

> O mother dear, Jerusalem,
> When shall I come to thee?
> When shall my sorrows have an end,
> Thy joys when shall I see?
> O happy harbor of the saints!
> O sweet and pleasant soil!
> In thee no sorrow may be found,
> No grief, no care, no toil.
>
> Thy gardens and thy goodly walks
> Continually are green,
> Where grow such sweet and pleasant flowers
> As nowhere else are seen.
> Right through the streets, with silver sound

The living waters flow;
And on the banks, on either side,
The trees of life do grow.

WHAT DOES HEAVEN SOUND LIKE?

In modern films, heaven is as hushed as a library. However, the Bible suggests that heaven is quite noisy! For example, the prophet Ezekiel (1:24) says of the angels ministering to God: "I heard the noise of their wings, like the noise of great waters, as the voice of the Almighty, the voice of speech, as the noise of a host."

Both the Bible and Koran say there is constant music, singing, and shouting in heaven. The Koran speaks of the angel Israfel, "whose heart-strings are a lute, and who has the sweetest voice of all God's creatures." Isaiah 6:3 says that the angels shout to each other, "Holy, holy, holy, is the Lord of hosts: the whole world is full of his glory." And Revelation 7:12 quotes the angels as saying, "Blessing, and glory, and wisdom, and thanksgiving, and honor, and power, and might, be unto God for ever and ever."

The Apocalypse of Paul, a Christian work that is not included in the Bible, says that the soul of King David stands in heaven with a harp, singing psalms—and his voice fills the city. When he reaches the end of his psalm, the angels shout hallelujah, "so that the foundations of the city were shaken."

ARE THERE ANIMALS IN HEAVEN?

For many of us, heaven would hardly be heaven without pets. The Romans believed that in the Elysian fields, the righteous picnic and play while their horses graze nearby. Native Americans believed that in the spirit world, spirits of men hunt spirits of buffalo.

Robert Bontine Cunninghame-Graham, a Scottish writer and politician, once wrote to Theodore Roosevelt, who was a noted sportsman: "God forbid that I should go to any heaven in which there are no horses."

There doesn't seem to be any mention in sacred scriptures, but presumably there must also be a heaven without animals for people who don't like pets!

ARE THERE BUILDINGS IN HEAVEN?

Since Revelation 21 speaks of the new Jerusalem coming down from heaven, heaven must have buildings. The heavenly city has a foundation "garnished with all manner of precious stones," twelve gates of pearl, and streets of gold. But it has no temple—"for the Lord God Almighty and the Lamb are the temple of it."

A number of people who have had near-death experiences say that they saw glorious buildings when they were in heaven, often towers like skyscrapers, in which souls lived and worked.

IS THERE ELECTRICITY IN HEAVEN?

In his vision of God's throne, Ezekiel says (1:27) that he saw something that looked like *khashmal*. The King James Version translates this Hebrew word "as the color of amber." The Revised English Bible translates it as "what might have been brass." But the Jewish Publication Society translation reads *khashmal* this way: "as the color of electrum." While scholars obviously don't agree about what Ezekiel saw, in modern Hebrew *khashmal* means "electricity."

Literally, lightning is a form of electricity. And this is why it was said of Benjamin Franklin that "he snatched lightning from heaven."

DOES GOD LIVE IN HEAVEN?

From earliest times, people believed that God lives in heaven. Many people believed—and still believe—that there are numerous sacred spirits—"gods"—who rule over specific domains: the earth, sea, sky, sun, moon, stars, trees, crops, animals, fertility, and more. In many cases, these spirits are pictured as little more than powerful humans, vulnerable to pain, limited in their scope, perhaps even subject to birth and death. But as the belief grew that gods are better than humans, people began to imagine them as higher than or above the human sphere. The Greeks put their gods on top of a high mountain, Mount Olympus. The ancient Indo-Europeans—the ancestors of most of the peoples of Europe and many of those in India and Persia—placed their main god in the sky, and called him

"Dyeus," from the word meaning "sky." From this name, Latin derives the word *deus* ("god"), as well as the names *Jove* and *Jupiter* (from *Jove-pater*, "father Jove"), Greek derives *Zeus*, and English derives *Tiw* (memorialized in *Tuesday*, "Tiw's day").

The Bible, of course, clearly tells us numerous times that God lives in heaven. Psalm 115:16 makes the point very neatly: "The heaven, even the heavens, are the Lord's: but the earth hath he given to the children of men." Likewise, Isaiah 66:1 says, "Thus saith the Lord, The heaven is my throne, and the earth is my footstool."

Nevertheless, the great monotheistic religions long ago realized that God cannot be contained in one place, no matter how expansive. As King Solomon observes in 2 Chronicles 6:18: "But will God in very deed dwell with men on the earth? behold, heaven and the heaven of heavens cannot contain thee; how much less this house which I have built!"

WHAT IS THE THRONE OF GOD?

Detailed descriptions of God's throne appear in both Ezekiel and Revelation. In the beginning of the book of Ezekiel, the prophet says that the "hand of the Lord" was upon him and he had a vision of heaven. In this vision he sees strange creatures, and "there was a voice from the firmament that was over their heads, when they stood, and had let down their wings. And above the firmament that was over their heads was the likeness of a throne, as the appearance of a sapphire stone. . ." (1:25–26).

In Revelation, John sees a door open in heaven and he, too, observes the throne of God:

And immediately I was in the spirit; and, behold, a throne

was set in heaven, and one sat on the throne. . . . and there was a rainbow round about the throne, in sight like unto an emerald. And round about the throne were four and twenty seats. . . . And out of the throne proceeded lightnings and thunderings and voices: and there were seven lamps of fire burning before the throne, which are the seven Spirits of God. And before the throne there was a sea of glass like unto crystal . . . (4:2-6).

WHAT DOES THE GLORY OF GOD LOOK LIKE?

In Ezekiel's vision, the glory of God appears on the heavenly throne. He says:

> . . . and upon the likeness of the throne was the likeness as the appearance of a man above upon it. And I saw as the color of amber, as the appearance of fire round about within it, from the appearance of his loins even upward, and from the appearance of his loins even downward, I saw as it were the appearance of fire, and it had brightness round about. As the appearance of the bow that is in the cloud in the day of rain, so was the appearance of the brightness round about. This was the appearance of the likeness of the glory of the Lord (1:26–28).

In John's vision in Revelation 4:2–3: ". . . a throne was set in heaven, and one sat on the throne. And he that sat was to look upon like a jasper and a sardine stone. . . ."

WHAT IS GOD'S CHARIOT?

Psalm 18:9–10 says that God "bowed the heavens also, and came down: . . . And he rode upon a cherub, and did fly."

In Ezekiel 1:5–14, the prophet sees four creatures beneath the firmament on which God's throne rests.

> And this was their appearance; they had the likeness of a man. And every one had four faces, and every one had four wings. And their feet were straight feet; and the sole of their feet was the sole of a calf's foot: and they sparkled like the color of burnished brass. . . . As for the likeness of their faces, they four had the face of a man, and the face of a lion, on the right side: and they four had the face of an ox on the left side; they four also had the face of an eagle. . . . And they went every one straight forward: whither the spirit was to go, they went; . . . And the living creatures ran and returned as the appearance of a flash of lightning.

So far, the living creatures are recognizable to us as some kind of angel. But then Ezekiel continues (1:15, 18–20):

> Now as I beheld the living creatures, behold one wheel upon the earth by the living creatures, with his four faces. . . . As for their rings, they were so high that they were dreadful; and their rings were full of eyes round about them four. And when the living creatures went, the wheels went by them: and when the living creatures were lifted up from the earth, the wheels were lifted up. Whithersoever the spirit was to go, they went, thither was their spirit to go; and the wheels were lifted up over against them: for the spirit of the living creature was in the wheels.

In chapter 10, Ezekiel repeats much of this description and specifically calls the creatures cherubim (15–17):

> And the cherubim were lifted up. This is the living creature that I saw . . . . And when the cherubim went, the wheels went by them: and when the cherubim lifted up their wings to mount up from the earth, the same wheels also turned not from beside them. When they stood, these stood; and when they were lifted up, these lifted up themselves also; for the spirit of the living creature was in them.

This vision is known in Hebrew as *Ma'aseh Merkavah* (The Story of the Chariot). Difficult as it is to interpret, it became a central motif in medieval Jewish mysticism.

DID JESUS LIVE IN HEAVEN BEFORE COMING TO EARTH?

The Bible tells us where Jesus went after his death. The Gospel of Mark says: "So then after the Lord had spoken unto them, he was received up into heaven, and sat on the right hand of God" (16:19). Similarly, Luke says: "And it came to pass, while he blessed them, he was parted from them, and carried up into heaven" (24:51). And in 1 Peter 3:22, we find: "[Jesus] Who is gone into heaven, and is on the right hand of God; angels and authorities and powers being made subject unto him."

But other passages add that Jesus was also in heaven before he was born. The Gospel of John equates Jesus with the Word that existed with God: "In the beginning was the Word, and the Word was with God, and the Word was God. The same was in the beginning with God. . . . And the Word was made flesh, and dwelt among us . . ." (1:1–2, 14). So too, in 3:13, John quotes Jesus as saying, "And no man hath ascended up to heaven, but he that came down from heaven, even the Son of man which is in heaven." And again in 6:38 Jesus says, "For I came down from heaven, not to do mine own will, but the will of him that sent me."

DO ANGELS LIVE IN HEAVEN?

The visions of the throne of God in the books of Ezekiel and Revelation clearly place angels in heaven. Revelation 7:11, one of numerous references to angels in the book, describes how "all the angels stood round about the throne . . . and fell before the throne on their faces, and worshipped God." In verse 14:6, John says, "And I saw another angel fly in the midst of heaven . . . ."

In addition, Genesis 21:17 states that ". . . the angel of God called to Hagar out of heaven." Genesis 22:15 says, "And the angel of the Lord called unto Abraham out of heaven . . . ."

Finally, the heavenly choir is composed of angels. Isaiah 6:2–3 describes the seraphim who cry one to the other, "Holy, holy, holy, is the Lord of hosts . . . ."

DOES SATAN LIVE IN HEAVEN?

According to evidence in the Bible, Satan once lived in heaven. But because he rebelled against God, he was thrown out.

In Job 1:6, Satan is among those who visit God's court:

"Now there was a day when the sons of God came to present themselves before the Lord, and Satan came also among them." But in Revelation 12:7–9 we read: "And there was war in heaven: Michael and his angels fought against the dragon . . . . And the great dragon was cast out, that old serpent, called the Devil, and Satan . . . ."

Nevertheless, in 2 Enoch, chapter 18, Satan and the rebellious angels are imprisoned—not in the depths of the earth or the dark pit but in the fifth heaven.

DO SOULS OF THE DEAD LIVE IN HEAVEN?

In the Judeo-Christian tradition as in many others, souls of the righteous dead go to heaven. Psalm 91:1 says that the righteous person "shall abide under the shadow of the Almighty." And Revelation 7:9–10 reports: "After this I beheld, and lo, a great multitude, which no man could number, of all nations, and kindreds, and people, and tongues, stood before the throne, and before the Lamb, clothed with white robes, and palms in their hands; And cried with a loud voice, saying, Salvation to our God which sitteth upon the throne, and unto the Lamb."

Bernard of Cluny, a Benedictine monk who lived during the twelfth century, expressed in the poem "Jerusalem the Golden" his belief that the righteous are rewarded in heaven. As in many other poems and hymns, the holy city of Jerusalem stands for heaven.

Jerusalem the golden,
With milk and honey blest!
Beneath thy contemplation

Sink heart and voice oppressed:
I know not, O I know not,
What joys await us there;
What radiancy of glory,
What bliss beyond compare.

They stand, those halls of Zion,
All jubilant with song,
And bright with many an angel,
And all the martyr throng:
The Prince is ever in them;
The daylight is serene;
The pastures of the blessed
Are decked in glorious sheen.

There is the throne of David,
And there, from care released,
The shout of them that triumph,
The song of them that feast;
And they who with their Leader,
Have conquered in the fight,
Forever and forever
Are clad in robes of white.

O sweet and blessed country,
The home of God's elect!
O sweet and blessed country,
That eager hearts expect!
Jesus, in mercy bring us
To that dear land of rest,
Who art, with God the Father,
And Spirit, ever blest.

(translated in the mid-1800s by J. M. Neale).

DO SOULS OF THE UNBORN LIVE IN HEAVEN?

Many people believe they do. Here is the logic: Since souls are immortal they never die. But can an immortal soul be born? How? The physical act of conception cannot create an immortal spirit. It follows, then, that all souls must have been created at the beginning of time, along with angels and other immortal creations. But where do these souls stay until it is time for them to enter a human body? The answer? In heaven.

This belief fits neatly with Plato's theory of ideas, which states that true knowledge is not learned but remembered by the soul from its pure spirit stage. The belief also coincides with the view of the eighteenth- and nineteenth-century philosophy known as romanticism, which emphasized our spiritual bond with nature. The great English poet William Wordsworth, for example, speaks of the newborn child as "trailing clouds of glory . . . from God, who is our home."

CHAPTER NINE

WHAT IS HELL LIKE?

WHAT WORDS DOES THE BIBLE USE FOR HELL?

The King James Version uses the word *hell* to translate two Hebrew words and two Greek words. The Hebrew word *Sheol* is translated as *hell* in many places, for example in Psalm 9:17: "The wicked shall be turned into hell, and all the nations that forget God." In Psalm 18:5, "The sorrows of hell compassed me about. . . ." However, *sheol* is rendered other ways as well. It is translated as *the grave* in Psalm 30:3: "O, Lord, thou hast brought up my soul from the grave," and in 49:15, "But God will redeem my soul from the power of the grave. . . ." And it is called *the pit* in Numbers 16:30, "But if the Lord make a new thing, and the earth open her mouth . . . and they go down quick into the pit," and in Job 17:16, "They shall go down to the bars of the pit . . . ."

Hell is also the word the translators use for *Gehenna*, which in the New Testament is the Greek form of the Hebrew word *Gehinnom*. For example, Matthew 5:29 says, "And if thy right eye offend thee, pluck it out, and cast it from thee: for it is profitable for thee that one of thy members should perish, and not that thy whole body should be cast into hell."

The Greek word *Hades* is translated as *hell* in Luke 12:5: "Fear him, which after he hath killed hath power to cast into hell." And the word *Tartaros* is rendered as *hell* in 2 Peter 2:4: "God spared not the angels that sinned, but cast them down to hell."

HOW MANY TIMES DOES JESUS MENTION HELL?

According to Strong's *Exhaustive Concordance of the Bible*, Jesus mentions the word hell sixteen times in the translation of the King James Version. In addition to Matthew 5:29 and Luke 12:5, quoted above, there is also this passage in Matthew 16:18: "And I say also unto thee, That thou art Peter, and upon this rock I will build my church; and the gates of hell shall not prevail against it." In Revelation 1:18, there is yet another mention of hell: "I am he that liveth, and was dead; and, behold, I am alive for evermore, Amen; and have the keys of hell and of death."

IS HELL A PLACE?

The passages we have been quoting certainly convey the idea that hell is a place one goes to or is cast down to. But hell is not necessarily a single place. Christopher Marlowe writes in *Dr. Faustus:*

When all the world dissolves,
And every creature shall be purified,
All places shall be hell that are not heaven.

Moreover, there are those—even among devout Christians—
who believe that hell is an emotion or a state of mind. Again, in
Dr. Faustus, Marlowe has one of the damned say:

Hell hath no limits, nor is circumscribed
In one place; for where we are is Hell,
And where Hell is, there must we ever be.

Similarly, John Milton says in his great epic *Paradise Lost:*

The mind is its own place, and in itself
Can make a heaven of hell, a hell of heaven.

And he has Satan say, "which way I fly is hell; myself am hell."

IS HELL IN THE CENTER OF THE EARTH?

Revelation 11:7 speaks of the "bottomless pit." Mark 9:43 says
that hell has "the fire that never shall be quenched." And
Revelation 9:1–2 puts both images together: "to him was given
the key to the bottomless pit. And he opened the bottomless pit;
and there arose a smoke out of the pit, as the smoke of a great furnace, and the sun and the air were darkened by reason of the
smoke of the pit." From what ancient people knew of volcanos
and from what we know of geology, this description of hell match-
es what we think of when we picture the center of the earth.

IS HELL A SEPARATE PART OF HEAVEN?

Rather than thinking of hell as deep in the earth, or as a bottomless pit out in space, or even as a separate place, some people think of hell as part of heaven. For example, in 2 Enoch, one hell—the place of eternal punishment for wicked people—is located in a section of the second heaven; another hell—for fallen angels—is located in the fifth heaven.

WHERE ARE THE GATES OF HELL?

Ancient people thought that volcanos—with their billowing smoke, continuous flames, and periodic bursts of fire and molten rock—were the gates of hell. In the *Aeneid*, Virgil tells us that the path leading to the gates of hell is at a place the Greeks call *Avernus*, meaning "no birds"; the fire, smoke, and heat make it impossible for birds to fly overhead. In a clever satire on evil, the twentieth-century American poet Vachel Lindsay places the gate to hell in Simon Legree's basement. He was the vicious slave owner in *Uncle Tom's Cabin*.

WHO SITS OUTSIDE THE GATES OF HELL?

According to a Jewish legend preserved in *Genesis Rabbah* (a collection of midrash, or commentary, on Genesis), chapter 48:8, the patriarch Abraham sits at the gates of hell. There, he protects those who are circumcised from being forced to enter. Both Jews and Muslims trace the ritual of circumcision to Abraham; in Hebrew the ritual is called "the covenant of Abraham our father."

WHAT DOES HELL LOOK LIKE?

Hell is a place of darkness (Matt. 8:12) and eternal fire (Mark 9:43). Even the water in hell is on fire (Apocalypse of Paul).

Shakespeare's sonnet 147 contains the line, "black as hell, as dark as night." And in what may be an insult either to hell or to London, Percy Bysshe Shelley wrote:

Hell is a city much like London—
A populous and smoky city.

In *Paradise Lost*, John Milton gives this description of what the fallen angels found when they explored hell:

. . . through many a dark and dreary Vale
They passed, and many a Region dolorous,
O'er many a Frozen, many a Fiery Alp,
Rocks, Caves, Lakes, Fens, Bogs, Dens, and shades of death,
A Universe of death, which God by curse
Created evil. . . .

101

IS HELL HOT OR COLD?

It's both. Hell not only contains eternal fire like a furnace but eternal ice as well. The Apocalypse of Paul describes a "place of ice and snow" where those who injured widows and orphans lie naked as their hands and feet are chopped off.

As John Milton explains in *Paradise Lost:*

. . . the parching Air
Burns frore, and cold performs th' effect of Fire.
Thither by harpy-footed Furies hal'd,
At certain revolutions all the damn'd
Are brought: and feel by turns the bitter change
Of fierce extremes, extremes by change more fierce,
From beds of raging Fire to starve in Ice. . . .

IS THERE WATER IN HELL?

Yes, but unfortunately, the water is on fire. Revelation speaks of a "lake of fire burning with brimstone." The Koran says that souls condemned to the fires of hell will be forced to drink boiling water. And the Apocalypse of Paul describes in excruciating detail the torment that will befall souls in the "river of fire burning with heat."

ARE THERE ANIMALS IN HELL?

There are beasts and monsters, but no pets! The most frequently mentioned hell-dwelling animal is the devouring worm, as in Mark 9:44, "their worm dieth not . . . ."

WHO RULES IN HELL?

Hell is the domain of Satan, also called the devil, as in Revelation 12:9: "the great dragon . . . that old serpent, called the Devil, and Satan . . . ."

After their rebellion in heaven, Satan and his cohorts were cast into hell as punishment. However, through a process that remains unclear, they came to "rule" hell. In *Paradise Lost*, John Milton explains that this, too, is a sign of their wickedness. Rather than repent and appeal to God for forgiveness, they choose to glory in their evil. As Satan explains:

> . . . Here at least
> We shall be free; th' Almighty hath not built
> Here for his envy, will not drive us hence:
> Here we may reign secure, and in my choice
> To reign is worth ambition though in hell:
> Better to reign in hell, than serve in heaven.

DO DEMONS LİVE İN HELL?

As we've just seen, Satan and the other fallen angels were cast into hell. Revelation 20:10 says: "And the devil . . . was cast into the lake of fire and brimstone . . . and shall be tormented day and night for ever and ever." So too, Jude 1:6: "And the angels which kept not their first estate, but left their own habitation, he hath reserved in everlasting chains under darkness. . . ."

In hell, some of these angels became what we might call demons. When demons mated, their offspring were also demons.

DO SOULS OF THE WİCKED LİVE İN HELL?

If you can call that living!

According to many religious traditions, souls of the wicked are condemned to hell. Matthew 13:41–42 says: "The Son of man shall send forth his angels, and they shall gather out of his kingdom all things that offend, and them which do iniquity; And shall cast them into a furnace of fire: there shall be wailing and gnashing of teeth."

In the Koran, the wicked—also called the "Companions of the Left"—suffer in a place of "burning winds and boiling waters." The only shade comes from the thick smoke that blots out the sun, but it offers no relief from the heat.

WHAT WAS THE HARROWING OF HELL?

The earliest understanding of Hebrew *Sheol* and Greek *Hades*—as opposed to *Gehenna* and *Tartaros*—was that they were places where all the dead, both good and evil, went after death. As a belief in resurrection arose and spread, several issues needed to be clarified. First of all, what happened to the righteous dead while they were waiting for the resurrection? A second question asked by early Christians: How could there be salvation through Jesus for people who had died before he was crucified? One answer to the first question was that the righteous would wait in *Sheol* or *Hades* until the appointed time.

Yet another question arose concerning death and resurrection: What did Jesus do during the three days that he was "dead"? One possible answer was that, being divine, he was not really dead. Another answer was that since the human Jesus had been righteous in life and was now dead—at least for three days—he was in *Sheol* or *Hades,* awaiting resurrection with the other righteous dead.

Eventually, all of these issues were clarified by what is known as the "harrowing of hell." This is the belief that during the three days he was humanly dead, Jesus descended into the Underworld—Hebrew *sheol,* Greek *Hades,* English *hell*—and preached there to the righteous dead. Three days later, when Jesus ascended into heaven, he took some of the righteous—especially the Hebrew patriarchs—with him. This event is called the "descent into hell" or the "harrowing of hell."

CHAPTER TEN

HOW ARE THE SOULS OF THE DEAD JUDGED?

ARE THE DEAD JUDGED IN THE GRAVE?

According to Islam, yes. As explained in a creed formulated by the eleventh century mystic Abu Hamid al-Ghazali, two terrible beings named Munkar and Nakir make the dead person sit up in the grave. They then ask him, "Who is your Lord? What is your religion? Who is your prophet?" The correct answers, of course, are Allah, Islam, and Mohammed.

IS THERE A GREAT COURTROOM IN THE SKY?

According to both Jewish and Christian views, the soul is judged at the throne of God—that is, in something like a courtroom in heaven. The classic description of this process appears in Zechariah 3:1–3:

> And he shewed me Joshua the high priest standing before the angel of the Lord, and Satan standing at his right hand to resist him. And the Lord said unto Satan, The Lord rebuke thee, O Satan; even the Lord that hath chosen Jerusalem rebuke thee: is not this a brand plucked out of the fire? Now Joshua was clothed with filthy garments, and stood before the angel. . . .

WHAT KINDS OF QUESTIONS DO THEY ASK THE DEAD?

As we have already seen, Islam teaches that the key questions are: Who is your Lord? What is your religion? Who is your prophet?

Judaism teaches that the name of your religion does not matter. Rather, the important questions focus on ethical behavior: Have you clothed the naked? Have you fed the hungry?

In Christianity, there are two kinds of key questions. For example, there are questions concerning religion: "Are you washed in the blood of the Lamb?" And there are questions about behavior, as in the parable of the lord who gives money to his servants for safekeeping:

> And unto one he gave five talents, to another two, and to another one . . . . Then he that had received the five talents went and traded with the same, and made them other five talents. And likewise he that had received two . . . . But he that had received one went and digged in the earth, and hid his lord's money. After a long time the lord . . . reckoneth with them. And so he that had received five talents came and brought other five talents . . . . His lord said unto him, Well done, thou good and faithful servant . . . . He also that had received two talents came . . . . His lord said unto him, Well done, good and faithful servant . . . . Then he which had received the one talent came . . . . His lord answered and said unto him, Thou wicked and slothful servant . . . ." (Matt. 25:15–26)

In other words, God will question us to see how we have used the abilities, skills, and other gifts that he has placed in our care during our life.

WHAT ARE THE REALLY BAD CRIMES?

In Islam the really bad crimes are religious: honoring the wrong god, professing the wrong faith. In Judaism the really bad crimes are ethical, as the prophets note many times: oppressing the widow and orphan; cheating workers; perverting justice. Christianity teaches that not accepting Jesus as the Christ is a major sin. In addition, there are the seven deadly sins: pride, wrath, envy, lust, gluttony, avarice, and sloth.

WILL SOMEONE COME FORWARD TO SPEAK FOR ME?

In Zechariah 3, God defends Joshua against the accusations of Satan. In the section of the Mishnah (the earliest section of the Talmud) called Ethics of the Fathers, Judaism teaches that good deeds create advocates on our behalf: "Each good deed a person does creates an advocate on his behalf. Each transgression creates an accuser. Thus, repentance and good deeds are a shield against calamity."

According to the Apocalypse of Paul, the archangel Michael stands before God and prays continually for all humankind. And even though he reproves sinners who have not lived properly on earth, nonetheless he prays for them when the time comes.

DO I HAVE TO CONFESS EVERYTHING?

You might as well, because the court has evidence. In Ethics of the Fathers, Rabbi Judah the Prince says, "Remember three things and you will stay away from sin: Above you is an eye that sees, an ear that hears, and all your actions are recorded in a book."

The record book figures also in the Apocalypse of Paul. When a soul tries to lie, God gets very angry and calls the angel who is in charge of that soul. The angel comes forward with a record book and begins to read all the sins the soul has committed since the age of fifteen. God stops the angel and says, "Just tell me the sins of the last five years. Did he repent and change his ways?"

Returning, then, to the words of Rabbi Judah: "Against your will you are born; against your will you die; and against your will you will give a reckoning to the King of Kings."

WHAT HAPPENS TO SİNNERS İN THE HANDS OF AN ANGRY GOD?

The Bible does not go into great detail about the punishment of the wicked. Punishment is threatened, and it is assured. But nothing in the Bible seems to take pleasure in describing the punishment. This is not so in later Christian and Islamic writings. The Apocalypse of Paul contains pages and pages of the most hideous tortures. The Puritans of the seventeenth and eighteenth centuries followed in this tradition. In a sermon entitled "Sinners in the Hands of an Angry God," Jonathan Edwards writes:

> The God that holds you over the pit of hell, much as one holds a spider, or some loathsome insect over the fire, abhors you, and is dreadfully provoked: his wrath towards you burns like fire; he looks upon you as worthy of nothing else, but to be cast into the fire. . . you are ten thousand times more abominable in his eyes, than the most hateful venomous serpent is in ours. . . . [I]t is a great furnace of wrath, a wide and bottomless pit, full of the fire of wrath . . . . You hang by a slender thread, with the flames of divine wrath flashing about it, and ready every moment to singe it, and burn it asunder . . . .

And in "The Future Punishment of the Wicked Unavoidable and Intolerable," Edwards writes:

> Imagine yourself to be cast into a fiery oven, all of a glowing heat, or into the midst of a glowing brick-kiln, or of a great furnace, where your pain would be much greater than that occasioned by accidently touching a coal of fire, as the heat is greater. Imagine also that your body were to lie there a quarter of an hour, full of fire, as full within and without as a bright coal of fire, all the while full of quick sense. . . . [H]ow long would that quarter of an hour seem to you! . . . O, then, how would your heart sink, if you thought, if you knew, that you must bear it forever and ever! That there would be no end!

İS MY SENTENCE DETERMİNED BY JUSTİCE OR MERCY?

Both, apparently. In Matthew 18:23–35, in the parable of the debtor, the key is justice. The king is willing to forgive the servant his debt; but when he discovers that the servant has sent his own debtor to prison for a much smaller sum, the king reinstates the debt. In an act of justice, he does to the servant what the servant had done to someone else.

However, in Matthew 20:1–15, in the parable of the laborers in the vineyard, the key element is mercy. The owner hires workers at different times of the day, but agrees to the same wages at each hiring. When those who were hired first complain that they have worked longer for the same wages as those who worked less, the owner replies that each got the wage he had agreed to. And if the owner overpaid the workers who worked least, how does this injure the others?

As the nineteenth-century poet James Russell Lowell notes:

'Tis heaven alone that is given away;
'Tis only God may be had for the asking.

HOW DOES THE PUNISHMENT FIT THE CRIME?

Many descriptions of hell emphasize that punishment is fashioned to fit the nature of the crime, not only in severity but also in spirit. For example, the Apocalypse of Peter says that blasphemers are hanged by the tongue; women who adorned themselves for adultery are hanged by the hair; murderers are torn by beasts; persecutors of the righteous are burned in a lake of fire; gossips must eat their own lips; those who refused to help the poor must live for eternity in filthy rags. And so on.

WHAT HAPPENS AT THE END OF THE TRIAL?

The results of the trial are described in this hymn by William Walker, composed in the 1830s:

High o'er the hills the mountains rise,
Their summits tower toward the skies;
But far above them I must dwell,
Or sink beneath the flames of hell.

Oh, God! forbid that I should fall
And lose my everlasting all;
But may I rise on wings of love,
And soar to the blest world above.

There I must lie till that great day,
When Gabriel's awful trumpet shall say,
Arise, the judgment day is come,
When all must hear their final doom.

If not prepared, then I must go
Down to eternal pain and woe,
With devils there I must remain,
And never more return again.

But if prepared, Oh, blessed thought!
I'll rise above the mountain's top,
And there remain for evermore
On Canaan's peaceful, happy shore.

Then will I sing God's praises there,
Who brought me through my troubles here
I'll sing, and be forever blest,
Find sweet and everlasting rest.

WOULD A GOD OF LOVE REALLY DAMN ME TO HELL?

This question has tormented theologians for centuries. It seems that a lot of ordinary people are betting that God will relent. They see God as a parent who threatens and threatens but who finally gives his children rewards they don't really deserve—because, after all, they are children, and the parent loves them. Most theologians, however, work in the opposite direction: they assume that the Bible is serious about reward and punishment. Their job is to explain how a parent who loves a child will, indeed, go through with the punishment.

Jonathan Edwards, the eighteenth-century Puritan preacher, seemed to take pleasure in bursting the bubble of his congregation's complacency. He writes:

> Doth it seem to thee incredible, that God should be so utterly regardless of the sinner's welfare, as so to sink him into an infinite abyss of misery? Is this shocking to thee? And is it not at all shocking to thee, that thou shouldst be so utterly regardless as thou hast been of the honor and glory of the infinite God? It arises from thy foolish stupidity and senselessness, and is because thou hast a heart of stone, that thou art so senseless of thine own wickedness as to think thou hast not deserved such a punishment, and that it is so incredible that it will be inflicted upon thee.

And Pope John Paul II, in *Crossing the Threshold of Hope*, addresses the dilemma this way:

> Is not God who is Love also ultimate Justice? Can He tolerate these terrible crimes, can they go unpunished? Isn't final punishment in some way necessary in order to reestablish moral equilibrium in the complex history of humanity? . . . It is Love that demands purification.

WHO IS ROCKED IN THE BOSOM OF ABRAHAM?

Luke 16:19–31 tells of a rich man and a poor man, both of whom died. The rich man was sent to hell, from which he saw the poor man, some distance off, in the bosom of Abraham. This is usually interpreted to mean that the poor, who have suffered in this world through no fault of their own, are protected in the next life by Abraham. Since the poor man in the story is not described as righteous—if he had been, he ought to have been in heaven—the story is interpreted to mean that those who are not good enough for heaven or bad enough for hell rest in the bosom of Abraham.

Some Christian theologians equate the bosom of Abraham with purgatory. Still others say that unbaptized children are also rocked in the bosom of Abraham.

A relief on the facade of the Cathedral of Rheims depicts angels delivering souls to Abraham's bosom.

WHAT IS PURGATORY?

In Catholic teaching, purgatory is for souls who are not wicked enough to go to hell but also not righteous enough to go straight to heaven. In purgatory, these souls are purged of their sins through punishment. In this way, they're made ready for heaven.

The great sixteenth-century Catholic mystic John of the Cross, whose major work is a description of the "dark night of the soul," speaks of the "living flame of love." Pope John Paul II explains in *Crossing the Threshold of Hope* that his own view of purgatory was strongly influenced by these teachings: "God makes man pass through such an interior purgatory of his sensual and spiritual nature in order to bring him into union with Himself."

WHAT IS LIMBO?

Limbo is the border area of hell. In Dante's *The Divine Comedy*, it is the highest level of hell, meaning that it is the least painful, since torture increases as you go lower and lower. It is home to the souls of unbaptized children, the mentally defective, and righteous pagans, who have done nothing wrong but who have not accepted Jesus as Christ. In some views, limbo is where the Old Testament saints awaited the coming of Christ.

In 1274, the Council of Lyons declared as Church doctrine that limbo is a place of less punishment than other parts of hell. Later theologians taught that souls in limbo only suffer sadness because they know that they can never be in the presence of God.

The exact location and function of limbo were subjects of debate. In his *Summa Theologica,* Thomas Aquinas devotes a few pages to clarifying whether the limbo of infants, limbo of Old Testament saints, and bosom of Abraham are separate places.

CAN MY PRAYERS HELP THOSE IN PURGATORY OR IN HELL?

Judaism teaches that souls go to a hell-like place for nearly a year to be purified, and then enter heaven. Part of their punishment is the fear that they have been pushed aside and forgotten. Therefore, the family of the dead person says the Kaddish (Sanctification of God) prayer on his or her behalf. The prayer is not *for* the dead, but *in memory of* the dead. It is recited daily only for eleven months, so as not to imply that the deceased needed a full year for purification.

The post-biblical Christian work, Apocalypse of Paul, says that the archangel Michael prays for humankind and, when asked, specifically for condemned souls.

ONCE YOU ARE CONDEMNED TO HELL, DO YOU STAY THERE FOREVER?

That depends on whether the particular description of hell and punishment refers to the "first" death or to the "second" death. Those who are in hell after the first death may get out of hell at the Second Coming, or the final Judgment Day at the end of time. But those who are condemned after the Second Coming are there for eternity. A lot of effort has been expended in attempts to explain the numbers in Daniel and Revelation, but there is little agreement.

In the meantime, some good news is that souls in hell get a few days of reprieve. According to the Apocalypse of the

Virgin, the days of Pentecost are days of rest. According to the Apocalypse of Paul, there is a reprieve "on the day" that Jesus arose from the dead. Some people interpret this to mean Easter; others, more optimistically, take it to mean every Sunday.

CHAPTER ELEVEN

HOW CAN WE GET INTO HEAVEN?

IS THE ROAD TO HEAVEN EASY OR HARD?

As with all worthwhile things, getting to heaven requires effort. Shakespeare says in *Hamlet*:

Do not, as some ungracious pastors do,
Show me the steep and thorny way to heaven,
Whiles, like a puff'd and reckless libertine,
Himself the primrose path of dalliance treads.

HOW DOES ONE LAY UP TREASURE IN HEAVEN?

Luke 12:33 advises: "Sell that ye have, and give alms; provide yourselves bags which wax not old, a treasure in the heavens that faileth not."

WHAT ACTIONS GET YOU INTO HEAVEN?

The seven virtues: faith, hope, charity, prudence, justice, fortitude, and temperance.

According to the poet Vachel Lindsay, General William Booth, the Methodist evangelist who founded the Salvation Army, got into heaven by caring for the outcasts of society.

John Masefield writes in "The Everlasting Mercy":

. . . he who gives a child a treat
Makes joy-bells ring in Heaven's street,
And he who gives a child a home
Builds palaces in Kingdom come.

Cecily R. Hallack writes in "The Divine Office of the Kitchen" that, since she has no time for keeping vigils or

. . . storming Heaven's gates
Make me a saint by getting meals
and washing up the plates.

Finally, prayer helps. Playwright John Webster says in the *Duchess of Malfi*:

Heaven-gates are not so highly arch'd
As prince's palaces; they that enter there
Must go upon their knees.

WHAT ACTIONS GET YOU INTO HEAVEN, ACCORDING TO THE BIBLE?

In addition to those mentioned in the previous answer, the Bible offers these courses of action:

"Blessed are ye, when men shall revile you, and persecute you, and shall say all manner of evil against you falsely, for my sake. Rejoice, and be exceeding glad: for great is your reward in heaven" (Matt. 5:11–12).

"For whosoever shall give you a cup of water to drink in my name, because ye belong to Christ, verily I say unto you, he shall not lose his reward" (Mark 9:41).

"Blessed is the man that endureth temptation: for when he is tried, he shall receive the crown of life, which the Lord hath promised to them that love him" (James 1:12).

"Feed the flock of God which is among you, taking the oversight thereof, not by constraint, but willingly, not for filthy lucre, but of a ready mind. . . . And when the chief Shepherd shall appear, ye shall receive a crown of glory that fadeth not away" (1 Pet. 5:2–4).

". . . be thou faithful unto death and I will give thee a crown of life" (Rev. 2:10).

"Finally, brethren, whatsoever things are true, whatsoever things are honest, whatsoever things are just, whatsoever things are pure, whatsoever things are lovely, whatsoever things are of good report; . . . Those things, which ye have both learned, and received, and heard, and seen in me, do: and the God of peace shall be with you" (Phil. 4:8–9).

HOW DOES THE SOUL GET TO HEAVEN?

Islam teaches that the soul must cross a bridge over hell in order to get to heaven. As Abu Hamid al-Ghazali states in his creed, after the soul is tested in the grave, its deeds are weighed in the balance, and then it must cross the bridge over hell. The bridge is sharper than a sword and narrower than a hair. The feet of the wicked slip, and they plunge into hell. The feet of the righteous are supported by the grace of God, and they reach heaven.

John Norris, a seventeenth-century poet, believed that the soul launched out on its own in an attempt to reach heaven:

The soul stands shivering on the ridge of life;
With what a dreadful curiosity
Does she launch out into the sea of vast eternity.

But Shakespeare says that the soul gets help. In *Henry VIII*, he writes:

Go with me, like good angels, to my end;
. . . .
And lift my soul to heaven.

DO UNBAPTIZED BABIES GET INTO HEAVEN?

This question bothered Christians almost from the beginning. After all, the babies hadn't done anything wrong, but nevertheless they still had the taint of original sin. Some theologians held the optimistic opinion that children who die unbaptized enjoy eternal life even if they cannot enter the Kingdom of God. Augustine, however, argued that only those who have accepted Jesus as Christ can go to heaven. Although this became the accepted teaching of the early Church, it is usually interpreted in the nicest way possible. Thus, one view is that unbaptized children are rocked in the bosom of Abraham. Another is that they are consigned to limbo, the least painful level of hell.

WHAT CAN YOU TAKE WITH YOU?

Nothing but the record of your good deeds. That is why Jesus says, "go and sell that thou hast, and give to the poor, and thou shalt have treasure in heaven" (Matt. 19:21).

DO THE POOR IN SPIRIT
GET INTO HEAVEN?

Yes. The Beatitudes (Matt. 5) begin with the words: "Blessed are the poor in spirit: for theirs is the kingdom of heaven."

As for the poor in wealth, the English novelist William Makepeace Thackeray observed, "Heaven does not choose its elect from among the great and wealthy."

CAN RICH PEOPLE BUY THEIR WAY INTO HEAVEN?

Not likely. Jesus said, "It is easier for a camel to go through the eye of a needle, than for a rich man to enter into the kingdom of God" (Mark 10:25). And lest anyone think that God can be bribed to look the other way, Deuteronomy 10:17 reminds us that ". . . the lord your God is God of gods, and Lord of lords, a great God, a mighty, and a terrible, which regardeth not persons, nor taketh reward"—meaning bribery.

WHO ABSOLUTELY CANNOT GET INTO HEAVEN?

Even though God is merciful and full of charity toward his creations, every religion recognizes sins that God simply cannot overlook. Among the more commonly cited ones are the denial of God, blasphemy, and drawing others into sin.

ONCE YOU ARE ADMITTED TO HEAVEN, DO YOU STAY THERE FOREVER?

Those who go to heaven before the Final Judgment do not necessarily stay there. Revelation 20:4 says that those who suffered violence while they witnessed for Jesus "lived and reigned with Christ a thousand years." After the thousand years, "the first resurrection" would come. As 1 Thessalonians 4:16–17 says, ". . . the dead in Christ shall rise first. Then we which are alive and remain shall be caught up together with them in the clouds, to meet the Lord in the air: and so shall we ever be with the Lord."

CHAPTER TWELVE

WHAT GOES ON IN HEAVEN?

WHAT DO ANGELS LOOK LIKE?

It is entirely possible that angels do not "look like" anything. Being spirits, they have no bodies in the physical sense. However, when angels are seen by humans, they must be seen in a shape. Different people have reported seeing different kinds of angels, either because their visions reflect their own experience or because there really *are* different kinds of angels.

The angels that appeared to Abraham in Genesis 18 looked like men, and so did the one that appeared to Samson's parents in Judges 13.

The cherubim described in Ezekiel 1 and 10 have four wings, straight feet, and soles "like the sole of a calf's foot." They sparkle like burnished brass. They have four faces—the face of a man, a lion, an ox, and an eagle. Wheels are attached to them in some way. "And their whole body, and their backs, and their hands, and their wings, and the wheels, were full of eyes round about" (10:12). Obviously, the chubby little baby cherubs of Renaissance paintings do not come from this vision!

The angel in Revelation 10 has a face like the sun, a rainbow on his head, and feet like pillars of fire.

WHAT DO ANGELS DO İN HEAVEN?

The word *angel* comes from a Greek word meaning "messenger." Angels appear to humans mainly to bring God's message. In addition, many religious traditions agree that angels take care of God's business and generally keep heaven running smoothly. They make the sun rise and set, control the seasons, usher souls from place to place, punish the wicked, sing in the heavenly choir, and generally minister to God.

HOW İS THE WORK OF HEAVEN ORGANİZED?

By collecting and collating details from many sources, scholars have pieced together a picture of the angelic hierarchy. In *The Book of Angels*, Carolyn Trickey-Bapty lists three angelic groups:

1. Seraphim, cherubim, thrones
2. Dominions, virtues, powers
3. Principalities, archangels, and angels

Each type of angel has a particular task. Powers, for example, are responsible for keeping order and controlling demons. Thrones administer justice.

WHO ARE THE MOST IMPORTANT ANGELS?

The archangels Michael, Gabriel, Raphael, and Uriel are the four "top" angels.

Michael, the dragon slayer, is the chief archangel. He led God's forces against Satan and the other rebellious angels.

Gabriel is the head of the heavenly guards and the Prince of Justice. According to Luke 1, Gabriel announced the births of John the Baptist and Jesus.

Raphael, whose name means "God heals," is in charge of healing and, therefore, science and knowledge.

Uriel controls thunder and the Underworld. Some legends say that he was the angel who kept Adam and Eve from reentering the Garden of Eden.

WHO MINISTERS AT GOD'S THRONE?

According to the vision of Isaiah (6:1–3): "I saw also the Lord sitting upon a throne, high and lifted up . . . . Above it stood the seraphim: each one had six wings; with twain he covered his face, and with twain he covered his feet, and with twain he did fly. And one cried unto another, and said, Holy, holy, holy, is the Lord of hosts: the whole earth is full of his glory."

In Ezekiel 1 and 10, the creatures with four faces and eye-studded bodies minister to God. In Revelation 4, four beasts and twenty-four elders minister to the throne:

And the first beast was like a lion, and the second beast like a calf, and the third beast had a face as a man, and the fourth beast was like a flying eagle. And the four beasts had each of them six wings about him; and they were full of eyes within: and they rest not day and night, saying, Holy, holy, holy, Lord God Almighty, which was, and is, and is to come. (4:7–8)

WHAT IS THE HEAVENLY CHOIR?

Several of the prophets in the Bible say that in their visions of heaven they heard angels singing praises to God. Isaiah, as we saw in the previous answer, observed seraphim singing, "Holy, holy, holy, is the Lord of hosts." Ezekiel, too, sees a vision of God's throne. When it is over, "the spirit took me up, and I heard behind me a voice of a great rushing, saying, Blessed be the glory of the Lord from his place" (3:12).

These and similar passages are given poetic expression in this hymn by Richard Mant, an eighteenth-century Irish cleric:

Round the Lord in glory seated,
Cherubim and seraphim
Filled His temple, and repeated
Each to each th' alternate hymn:

Lord, Thy glory fills the heaven,
Earth is with Thy fullness stored;
Unto Thee be glory given,
Holy, holy, holy Lord!

Heaven is with Thy glory ringing,
Earth takes up the angel cry,

"Holy, holy, holy," singing,
"Lord of Hosts, Thou Lord most high!"

Lord, Thy glory . . . .

With His seraph train before Him,
With His holy Church below,
Thus unite we to adore Him,
Bid we thus our anthem flow:

Lord, Thy glory . . . .

WHO GUARDS HEAVEN?

We have already seen that the archangel Michael leads
God's army, Gabriel is head of the guard, and Powers are
responsible for keeping order. As Henry Vaughan wrote in the
seventeenth century:

My soul, there is a country
Far beyond the stars
Where stands a winged sentry
All skilful in the wars.

However, according to the Marine Corps hymn:

If the Army and the Navy
Ever look on Heaven's scenes,
They will find the streets are guarded by
The United States Marines.

WAS THERE EVER A WAR IN HEAVEN?

Yes, according to the vision in Revelation 12:7–9:

. . . there was war in heaven: Michael and his angels fought against the dragon; and the dragon fought and his angels, And prevailed not; neither was their place found any more in heaven. And the great dragon was cast out, that old serpent, called the Devil, and Satan, which deceiveth the whole world.

WHAT DO SOULS DO IN HEAVEN?

Many people have wondered: What exactly do righteous souls *do* in heaven? Some people believe that heaven must be like an eternal picnic, where souls eat, drink, and sleep on the grass. Others say that righteous souls become members of the heavenly choir and sing praise to God. Still others believe that righteous souls experience bliss just basking in the presence of God.

The following hymn, composed by Reginald Heber and Richard Whately in the early nineteenth century, compares heavenly existence to peaceful sleep:

God, that madest earth and Heaven,
Darkness and light;
Who the day for toil hast given,
For rest the night;
May Thine angel guards defend us,

Slumber sweet Thy mercy send us;
Holy dreams and hopes attend us,
This livelong night.
Guard us waking, guard us sleeping;
And when we die,
May we in Thy mighty keeping
All peaceful lie.
When the last dread call shall wake us,
Do not Thou, our Lord, forsake us,
But to reign in glory take us,
With Thee on high.

WILL I BECOME AN ANGEL IN HEAVEN?

While the dead give up their physical bodies and exist only as spirits, they do not become angels. However, they do become angel-like in some ways. Angels are a separate form of creation, with their own traits, functions, and history.

WILL I BE YOUNG AND HEALTHY AGAIN?

This is a question that many people are anxious to have answered. Nobody, of course, wants to live forever in a broken or painful body. The dream of heaven is that the sick will be made well and the broken will be made whole. But this concept may be too literal. Since the soul is spirit, not material, it

135

probably doesn't age or lose a "limb" if the physical body suffers an accident. Perhaps souls are always young and healthy.

In any event, many religions and religious thinkers have tried to answer this question in different ways, but the final answer remains a mystery.

WILL ALL MY DREAMS COME TRUE IN HEAVEN?

The Irish poet Thomas Moore believed that "the heaven of each is but what each desires." Similarly, in *The Rubáiyát of Omar Khayyam*, Edward FitzGerald calls heaven

. . . but the Vision of fulfill'd Desire,
And Hell the Shadow from a Soul on fire.

And Robert Browning writes, "Things learned on earth, we shall practice in heaven." But, he said if life wasn't long enough to accomplish everything,

. . . a man's reach should exceed his grasp,
Or what's a heaven for?

ARE HEAVEN'S REWARDS SPIRITUAL OR SENSUAL?

Many religious books describe the rewards of heaven in physical terms. However, for thousands of years, religious thinkers have warned that these descriptions are merely poetic images that help us understand ideas beyond our understanding. These thinkers are content with the admittedly less explicit notion that the soul finds pleasure just being near God. Isaac Watts, an early eighteenth-century composer, expresses this concept in the following hymn:

> High in the heavens, eternal God,
> Thy goodness in full glory shines;
> Thy truth shall break through ev'ry cloud
> That veils and darkens Thy designs.
>
> My God, how excellent Thy grace,
> Whence all our hope and comfort spring!
> The sons of Adam in distress
> Fly to the shadow of Thy wing.
>
> Life, like a fountain rich and free,
> Springs from the presence of my Lord;
> And in Thy light our souls shall see
> The glories promised in Thy word.

WHAT DOES RESTING IN THE SHADOW OF GOD MEAN?

Rather than describe the rewards of heaven in terms of physical senses, many religious thinkers attempt a spiritual explanation. They say that the joy of heaven comes from the soul returning to its source, where it can bask in the embrace of God or be sheltered in the shadow of God's wing.

This idea is captured in a beautiful hymn from *The Foundry Collection*, a Wesleyan hymnbook published in 1742:

> Rise, my soul, and stretch thy wings,
> Thy better portion trace;

Rise from transitory things,
Toward heaven, thy destined place:
Sun and moon and stars decay,
Time shall soon this earth remove;
Rise, my soul, and haste away
To seats prepared above.

Rivers to the ocean run,
Nor stay in all their course;
Fire, ascending seeks the sun,
Both speed them to their source:
So a soul, that's born of God,
Pants to view His glorious face,
Upward tends to His abode,
To rest in His embrace.

Cease, my soul, oh, cease to mourn!
Press onward to the prize;
Soon the Saviour will return,
To take thee to the skies:
There is everlasting peace,
Rest, enduring rest, in heaven;
There will sorrow ever cease,
And crowns of joy be given.

A similar sentiment runs through this hymn, composed by Henry Francis Lyte in 1834. Drawing on the language of Psalm 84, the hymn compares the soul seeking God to the dove that flew out of Noah's ark searching for a place to rest:

Pleasant are Thy courts above,
In the land of light and love;
Pleasant are Thy courts below,
In this land of sin and woe.
O my spirit longs and faints

For the converse of Thy saints,
For the brightness of Thy face,
For Thy fullness, God of grace!

Happy birds that sing and fly
Round Thy altars, O Most High!
Happier souls that find a rest
In a heav'nly Father's breast!
Like the wandering dove that found
No repose on earth around,
They can to their ark repair
And enjoy it even there.

WILL I BE REUNITED WITH MY FRIENDS AND FAMILY IN HEAVEN?

From earliest times people have believed that in the afterlife they will be reunited with their departed family and friends. In fact, the Hebrew Bible frequently uses the phrase "gathered to his fathers" to describe death.

The fervent hope that we will once again see our loved ones is captured in this hymn by the eighteenth-century hymn writer John Cennick:

Children of the heavenly King,
As ye journey, sweetly sing;
Sing your Saviour's worthy praise,
Glorious in His works and ways.
We are traveling home to God
In the way the fathers trod;
They are happy now, and we
Soon their happiness shall see.

A similar hope is even more explicitly expressed in the following spiritual, which is believed to be from the early eighteenth century. Like many other spirituals, it sings of earthly freedom and eternal rest by retelling the story of the Israelite journey from Egyptian bondage to the promised land of Canaan:

Our bondage it shall end, by and by, by and by,
Our bondage it shall end, by and by.
From Egypt's yoke set free;
Hail the glorious jubilee.
And to Canaan we'll return, by and by, by and by,
And to Canaan we'll return, by and by.

And when to Jordan's flood, we are come, we are come,
And when to Jordan's flood, we are come,
Jehovah rules the tide,
And the waters he'll divide.
And the ransom'd host shall shout, "We are come, we are come."
And the ransom'd host shall shout, We are come."

Then friends shall meet again, who have loved, who have loved,
Then friends shall meet again, who have loved.
Our embraces will be sweet
At the dear Redeemer's feet,
When we meet to part no more, who have loved, who have loved,
When we meet to part no more, who have loved.

WİLL İ STİLL BE MARRİED TO MY SPOUSE?

This is another question that has troubled many people. In Mark 12:19–25, the hypothetical question is posed about a widow who remarried six times: "In the resurrection therefore, when they shall rise, whose wife shall she be of them? for the seven had her to wife." Jesus answers that "when they shall rise from the dead, they neither marry, nor are given in marriage; but are as the angels which are in heaven."

Mormons, however, believe that the family unit—spouse, children, siblings, relatives—prevails beyond the grave.

WİLL İ CARE ABOUT LOVED ONES WHO ARE STİLL ALİVE?

People sometimes explain ghosts as spirits of the dead who have come to help the loved ones they left behind. However, some people who have had near-death experiences and believe they went to heaven report that they no longer felt connected to this world.

WHAT IS THE ACADEMY OF HEAVEN?

Because Judaism places so much value on education, and because many scholars consider the study of Torah the greatest pleasure imaginable, the Talmud and other sources state that the righteous will be rewarded by continuing their studies in the Academy of Heaven.

DO SOULS WORK IN HEAVEN?

Many descriptions of heaven include *activities* that bring fulfillment to the soul: singing, learning, even weaving and planting. But there is no actual, "sweat of the brow" work in heaven.

On the other hand, some religious thinkers see heaven as an eternal Day of Rest. Or, to put it a different way, they see the Sabbath as a small taste of the life to come. This thought is expressed in the following Sabbath hymn by the eighteenth-century churchman John Newton:

> Safely through another week
> God has brought us on our way;
> Let us now a blessing seek,
> Waiting in His courts today;
> Day of all the week the best,
> Emblem of eternal rest;
> Day of all the week the best,
> Emblem of eternal rest.

Here we come, Thy name to praise,
Let us feel Thy presence near;
May Thy glory meet our eyes,
While we in Thy house appear;
Here afford us, Lord, a taste
Of our everlasting feast.
Here afford us, Lord, a taste
Of our everlasting feast.

DO SOULS EAT AND SLEEP IN HEAVEN?

In a physical sense, this isn't likely. But in a spiritual sense, it is. In Revelation 2:7, Jesus says, "To him that overcometh will I give to eat of the tree of life, which is in the midst of the paradise of God." So too, the Koran speaks of the wonderful food and relaxation waiting for the righteous. These visions of another dimension are clothed in language that humans can understand.

DO SOULS FEEL PLEASURE AND PAIN?

There couldn't be reward and punishment if souls couldn't feel. But these sensations cannot be physical; they must be experiences that the soul interprets as akin to bodily feelings of pleasure and pain.

In *Embraced by the Light*, an account of her near-death experience, Betty J. Eadie says she knew she was "dead" when she no longer felt the pain of her recent surgery.

143

DO MARRIED COUPLES HAVE SEX IN HEAVEN?

If there is no marriage and no giving in marriage, there are no married couples. Nonetheless, religions that believe couples *do* stay married also tend to believe that they engage in something similar to sex, only on a spiritual plane. In *Paradise Lost*, John Milton tries very hard to describe how this works. His attempt is worth reading!

HOW WILL THE DEAD BE MADE TO LIVE?

Most references to resurrection say simply that it will happen: the graves will open and the dead will rise. A more detailed picture occurs in Ezekiel 37:1–10:

> The hand of the Lord was upon me, . . . set me down in the midst of the valley which was full of bones. . . . And he said unto me, Son of man, can these bones live? And I answered, O Lord God, thou knowest. Again he said unto me, Prophesy upon these bones . . . . So I prophesied as I was commanded: and as I prophesied, there was a noise, and behold a shaking, and the bones came together, bone to his bone. And . . . the sinews and the flesh came up upon them, and the skin covered them above: but there was no breath in them. Then said he unto me, Prophesy unto the wind, prophesy, son of man, and say to the wind, Thus saith the Lord God; Come from the four winds, O

breath, and breathe upon these slain, that they may live. So I prophesied as he commanded me, and the breath came into them, and they lived, and stood up upon their feet . . . .

CHAPTER THIRTEEN

HOW DO PEOPLE WHO HAVE "DIED" AND COME BACK DESCRIBE HEAVEN?

WHAT IS A NEAR-DEATH EXPERIENCE?

Near-death experience is the name for what happens when a person who is declared medically dead is later revived. This condition may last several minutes or several hours. Some people who have had such experiences remember in elaborate detail what happened to them while they were "dead."

WHAT ARE THE MAJOR FEATURES THAT HAVE BEEN REPORTED?

Those who have collected and studied accounts of near-death experiences note that a number of features are reported again and again. According to Raymond Moody, in *Life After Life*, each near-death experience is unique. No experience seems to include all of the following features, but all of the experiences share several of them. No feature occurs in all cases, but each of them occurs in more than one case. Here is a list of the most important features of near-death experiences:

1. Ineffability. The experience is beyond human language. Whatever happened, it cannot be explained adequately in normal language. All attempts to talk about it are recognized by the speaker as weak approximations.

2. Hearing the News. The person is conscious of hearing medical personnel or others say that he or she is dead—and remembers thinking that they are mistaken.

3. Sounds. After dying, the person hears either painful noise or soothing music.

4. The Tunnel. People feel as if they are traveling, usually at great speed, through a dark tunnel.

5. Meeting Others. After leaving the tunnel, they meet other beings—sometimes people they know, sometimes spirits they have never seen.

6. The Being of Light. They meet a radiant spirit, usually described as warm and loving. Christians will often insist that this being is Jesus.

7. The Review. Something or someone guides them through a review of their lives.

IS DEATH PAINFUL?

As Raymond Moody points out, reports of near-death experiences are about *dying*, not about being dead, for such people are not *really* dead. As for whether *dying* is painful, Betty J. Eadie notes in *Embraced by the Light* that as soon as she "died," the pain of her recent surgery went away. Betty Malz reports in *My Glimpse of Eternity* that, despite painful incisions from an operation, she was able to walk without effort when she was "dead."

HOW DO THESE PEOPLE GET TO HEAVEN?

Many report flying at great speed through a dark tunnel and emerging into heaven at the end.

WHO GREETS THEM?

Some people say they were greeted by spirits, others by the "Being of Light." Betty Eadie reports something akin to a garden party: spirits in pastel gowns congratulated her on her "graduation" into the next stage of existence.

Betty Malz says that she cannot explain why, but she instinctively knew that the Being of Light was Jesus. So too,

George G. Ritchie recounts in *Return to Tomorrow* that he encountered "a Man made out of light," and "a kind of knowing" told him that this was Jesus.

DO THEY MEET PEOPLE THEY KNOW?

Some do, some don't. Betty Eadie reports meeting two old friends who were very happy to see her again. Others say that they were overcome by the wonder of their new surroundings and felt no interest in their previous existence.

Perhaps more interestingly, Betty Eadie says that spirits were making contacts with people in their future. One spirit was playing Cupid, trying to bring his future parents together on earth.

WHAT DO THESE RETURNED ONES SEE?

George Ritchie reports seeing a bright city made of light, very much like the one described in Revelation, which he had not even read. Betty Malz says she saw a silver structure like a palace and a gate made of pearl. Betty Eadie says she saw many buildings, including one which she describes as a library and another which was a workshop with looms.

ARE THEIR SOULS JUDGED?

Yes and no. Several people report that they reviewed their lives in detail, almost as if watching a video playback. Betty Eadie says that she was questioned by a council. But everyone seems to agree that nobody *judged* them: in their new state of pure knowledge, they judged their own lives and expressed shame or embarrassment at their errors. As George Ritchie says, "I realized that it was I who was judging . . . ."

WHY DO THESE SOULS COME BACK?

First, because it was not their time to die. Second, because they were told that they had work to finish.

In most cases, they were very happy in their new existence and did not want to come back. In some cases, they understood the importance of their mission on earth and wanted to return. However, once back, they did not always remember their mission, and had to work at recreating it.

HOW WERE THEIR LIVES AFFECTED BY SEEING HEAVEN?

People who have had near-death experiences and write books about it seem to be driven by religious motivations.

Regardless of what they were or believed before, they are now convinced that they know right from wrong and what God requires of them. Writing their books and sharing their knowledge is obviously part of their mission.

CHAPTER FOURTEEN

WHAT ARE SOME POPULAR HYMNS AND SPIRITUALS ABOUT HEAVEN AND THE AFTERLIFE?

AMAZING GRACE
(John Newton)
Amazing grace! how sweet the sound,
That saved a wretch like me!
I once was lost, but now am found,
Was blind but now I see.

Through many dangers, toils, and snares,
I have already come,
'Tis grace hath brought me safe thus far,
And grace will lead me home.

NEARER, MY GOD, TO THEE
(Sarah F. Adams)
Nearer, my God, to Thee,
Nearer to Thee!
E'en though it be a cross
That raiseth me;
Still all my song shall be,
Nearer, my God, to Thee,
Nearer to Thee.

Though like the wanderer,
The sun gone down,
Darkness be over me,
My rest a stone,
Yet in my dreams I'd be
Nearer, my God, to Thee,
Nearer to Thee.

There let the way appear,
Steps unto heaven;
All that Thou sendest me
In mercy given;
Angels to beckon me
Nearer, my God, to Thee,
Nearer to Thee.

IN THE SWEET BY AND BY
(S. Fillmore Bennett)
There's a land that is fairer than day,
And by faith we can see it afar,
For the Father waits over the way,
To prepare us a dwelling place there.

In the sweet by and by
We shall meet on that beautiful shore;
In the sweet by and by
We shall meet on that beautiful shore.

We shall sing on that beautiful shore
The melodious songs of the blest,
And our spirits shall sorrow no more,
Not a sigh for the blessing of rest.

In the sweet by and by . . . .

To our bountiful Father above
We will offer the tribute of praise
For the glorious gift of His love,
And the blessings that hallow our days.
In the sweet by and by . . . .

O GOD, OUR HELP IN AGES PAST
(Isaac Watts)
O God, our help in ages past,
Our hope for years to come,
Our shelter from the stormy blast,
And our eternal home.

Before the hills in order stood,
Or earth received her frame,
From everlasting Thou art God,
To endless years the same.

A thousand ages in Thy sight
Are like an evening gone;
Short as the watch that ends the night
Before the rising sun.

155

O God, our help in ages past,
Our hope for years to come,
Be Thou our Guide while life shall last,
And our eternal home.

FATHER AND FRIEND, THY LIGHT, THY LOVE
(Sir John Bowring)
Father and Friend! Thy light, Thy love,
Beaming through all Thy works we see;
Thy glory gilds the heavens above,
And all the earth is full of Thee.

Thy voice we hear, Thy presence feel,
Whilst Thou, too pure for mortal sight,
Involved in clouds, invisible,
Reignest the Lord of life and light.

We know not in what hallowed part
Of the wide heavens Thy throne may be,
But this we know, that where Thou art,
Strength, wisdom, goodness dwell with Thee.

Thy children shall not faint nor fear,
Sustained by this exalted thought:
Since Thou, their God, art everywhere,
They cannot be where Thou art not.

BEAUTIFUL ISLE OF SOMEWHERE
(Jessie B. Pounds)
(President McKinley's favorite song)
Somewhere the sun is shining,
Somewhere the song-birds dwell;
Hush, then, thy sad repining,
God lives, and all is well.

Somewhere, somewhere,
Beautiful Isle of somewhere!
Land of the true,
Where we live anew,
Beautiful isle of somewhere.

Somewhere the day is longer,
Somewhere the task is done;
Somewhere the heart is stronger,
Somewhere the guerdon won.

Somewhere. . . .
Somewhere the load is lifted,
Close by an open gate;
Somewhere the clouds are rifted,
Somewhere angels wait.

Somewhere. . . .

ROCK OF AGES
(Augustus Montague Toplady)
Rock of ages, cleft for me!
Let me hide myself in Thee;
Let the water and blood,
From Thy riven side which flowed,
Be of sin the double cure,
Cleanse me from its guilt and power.

Could my zeal no respite know,
Could my tears forever flow,
All for sin could not atone,
Thou must save, and Thou alone;
Nothing in my hand I bring,
Simply to Thy cross I cling.

While I draw this fleeting breath,
When mine eyelids close in death,
When I soar to worlds unknown,
And behold Thee on Thy throne,
Rock of ages, cleft for me,
Let me hide myself in Thee.

BEULAH LAND
(Edgar Page)
I've reached the land of corn and wine,
And all its riches freely mine;
Here shines undimmed one blissful day,
For all my night has passed away.

My Savior comes and walks with me,
And sweet communion here have we;
He gently leads me by His hand,
For this is heaven's borderland.

A sweet perfume up on the breeze
Is borne from ever-vernal trees,
And flowers that never fading grow
Where streams of life forever flow.

The zephyrs seem to float to me
Sweet sounds of heaven's melody,
As angels with the white-robed throng
Join in the sweet redemption song.

THERE IS A HAPPY LAND
(Andrew Young)
There is a happy land,
Far, far away,
Where saints in glory stand,

Bright, bright as day;
Oh, how they sweetly sing,
Worthy is the Saviour King,
Loud let His praises ring,
Praise, praise for aye.

Come to that happy land,
Come, come away;
Why will ye doubting stand,
Why still delay;
Oh, we shall happy be,
When from sin and sorrow free,
Lord, we shall dwell with thee,
Blest, blest for aye.

Bright in that happy land,
Beams every eye;
Kept by a Father's hand,
Love cannot die;
Oh, then, to glory run,
Be a crown and kingdom won,
And, bright above the sun,
Reign, reign for aye.

NOBODY KNOWS THE TROUBLE I'VE SEEN
Nobody knows the trouble I've seen,
Nobody knows but Jesus,
Nobody knows the trouble I've seen,
Glory, hallelujah.
Sometimes I'm up, sometimes I'm down,
Oh, yes, Lord,
Sometimes I'm almost to the ground,
Oh, yes, Lord.

Nobody knows . . . .

Although you see me going along so,
Oh, yes, Lord,
I have my trials here below,
Oh, yes, Lord.

Nobody knows . . . .

Once when I was walking along,
Oh, yes, Lord,
The element opened and the Lord came down,
Oh, yes, Lord.

Nobody knows . . . .

ROLL, JORDAN, ROLL
O brothers (O sisters),
You ought to have been there,
Yes, my Lord,
A-sitting in the Kingdom
To hear Jordan roll.

Roll, Jordan, roll,
Roll, Jordan, roll.
I want to go to heaven when I die
To hear Jordan roll.

THAT OLD TIME RELIGION
Give me that old time religion.
Give me that old time religion.
Give me that old time religion.
It's good enough for me.

It was good for our mothers. (3x)
And it's good enough for me.

It has saved our fathers. (3x)
And it's . . . .

It was good for the prophet Daniel. (3x)
And it's . . . .

It was good for the Hebrew children. (3x)
And it's . . . .

It was tried in the fiery furnace. (3x)
And it's . . . .

It will take us all to heaven. (3x)
And it's . . . .

SWING LOW, SWEET CHARIOT
Swing low, sweet chariot,
Coming for to carry me home.
Swing low, sweet chariot,
Coming for to carry me home.

I looked out over Jordan
And what did I see?
A band of angels
Coming after me.

Swing low . . . .

WHERE ARE THE HEBREW CHILDREN?
Where are the Hebrew children?
Where are the Hebrew children?
Where are the Hebrew children?
Safe in the promised land.
Though the furnace flamed around them,
God, while in their troubles found them,
He with love and mercy bound them,
Safe in the promised land.

Where are the twelve apostles? (3x)
Safe in the promised land.
They went up through pain and sighing,
Scoffing, scourging, crucifying,
Nobly for their master dying,
Safe in the promised land.

Where are the holy Christians? (3x)
Safe in the promised land.
Those who've washed their robes and made them
White and spotless pure and laid them
Where no earthly stain can fade them,
Safe in the promised land.

DIDN'T MY LORD DELIVER DANIEL
Didn't my Lord deliver Daniel, deliver Daniel,
Didn't my Lord deliver Daniel,
And why not every man?
He delivered Daniel from the lion's den,
Jonah from the belly of the whale,
And the Hebrew children from the fiery furnace,
And why not every man?

Didn't my Lord . . . .

The moon run down in a purple stream,
The sun forbear to shine,
And every star disappear,
King Jesus shall be mine.

Didn't my Lord . . . .

The wind blows East, and the wind blows West,
It blows like the Judgment Day,
And every poor soul that never did pray
Will be glad to pray that day.

Didn't my Lord . . . .

I set my foot on the Gospel ship,
And the ship it begin to sail,
It landed me over on Canaan's shore,
And I'll never come back any more.

Didn't my Lord . . . .

CHAPTER FIFTEEN

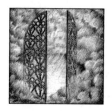

HOW HAS HEAVEN AFFECTED AMERICAN CULTURE?

ARE MANY TOWNS NAMED AFTER HEAVEN?

Given the importance of religion in the history of the United States, it's not surprising that more than a thousand towns and cities have biblical names. Almost every state has at least one town named after a biblical place. Half have Bethels; twenty have Goshens. Salem (short for Jerusalem) appears in two dozen places around the country. Bethlehem, Jericho, Bethesda, (New) Canaan—all are American towns. But few places are actually named *heaven*. Two of them are Heavenly Valley in California and Almost Heaven, a community of Christian militia in Idaho. Heavener, Oklahoma, almost counts, but it was really named after a local VIP.

Towns called Paradise, on the other hand, are nearly everywhere. Paradise, South Dakota, got its name when an unrelated man and woman named Adam and Eve settled near each other! On most other occasions, however, the name seems to reflect a secular thought: early settlers considered a certain place very beautiful, or a developer thought the name would be good for business. In one California town, locals claim that the original name was Pair o' Dice!

Some historians suggest that trappers, miners, and pioneers spoke profanity but avoided blasphemy. Maybe this explains why references to hell and the devil are so much more common than heaven. There were once many places named Hell, Hell Hole, and Hell Hollow, although the post office and real estate economics have reduced the number. Hell Hole Creek, South Carolina, commemorates a massacre during the Revolutionary War; Hell Canyon, Colorado, a near disaster in a storm. Hellgate, named by the Dutch skipper Adriaen Block in 1614, is a dangerous, narrow channel between New York City and Long Island. Legend has it that although Block referred to the swirling currents as Hell's Gate, others observed that the road to hell is wide and smooth.

Names that incorporate the word *devil* are often translations of Native American spirit names—for example, Devil's Lake in North Dakota and Devil Track Lake in Minnesota. Devil's Tower National Monument in Wyoming got its name from the Indian belief that bad spirits lived there. Most of the names originally coined in English were meant to be humorous rather than religious, often describing a forbidding or treacherous topography: Devil's Den, Devil's Canyon, and Devil's Postpile National Monument in California. Between the northern tip of Manhattan Island and the mainland there is a swirling eddy called Spuyten Duyvil. Some area residents say the name means "spitting devil" in Dutch. A more interesting explanation is that it got its name from an incident during the war between England and Holland in the seventeenth century. A Dutch soldier from New Amsterdam was trying to reach Yonkers and Tarrytown to get reinforcements. When told that the waters were too dangerous to cross, he replied that he would carry out his orders "spite the devil" and plunged in. He drowned, and New Amsterdam fell.

English-speaking settlers, being mostly Protestant, did not name many places after Purgatory. Purgatoire River in Colorado was originally named by the Spanish. In 1594 a group of Spanish explorers got lost and died without a priest present to administer last rites. The river where their remains were found was therefore named El Rio de las Animas Perdidas en Purgatorio, "The River of the Lost Souls in Purgatory." French trappers shortened the name to the current French form, Purgatoire. Because of their difficulty with the French pronunciation "purr-gaht-WAHR," American cowboys called it "Picketwire."

HOW MANY BOOKS HAVE BEEN WRITTEN ABOUT HEAVEN?

Heaven only knows! Under the subject heading "Heaven," *Books in Print* lists more than fifty books in English currently on the market, and advises the reader to check also under "Future Life," "Paradise," "Angels," "Beatific Vision," and "Intermediate State." Here are some sample titles:

Heaven: A Glimpse of Your Future Home
Heaven: What Would It Be Like to Talk to God about Heaven Here and Hereafter
Heaven: A Place, a City, a Home
Treasures in Heaven
I Saw Heaven
Heaven for Those Who Can't Believe
Where Exactly Is Heaven: Science, God and Common Sense

How to Get to Heaven
The Hope of Heaven: What Happens When We Die?
The Nature of Things to Come
God, Heaven and You
More Than Harps of Gold

The number of books on other subjects that have "heaven" in their titles further testifies to its importance in our culture:
Roots of Heaven, by Romain Gary
Heaven's My Destination, by Thornton Wilder
Fire from Heaven, by Mary Renault
Heaven and Hell, by Aldous Huxley
The Cat Who Went to Heaven, by Elizabeth Coatsworth
Second Heaven, by Judith Guest

And here are some non-theological examples of the two hundred or so books that use *heaven* as the first word in their titles:
Heavens to Betsy! And Other Curious Sayings
Heaven on Horseback
Heaven on Wheels
Heaven Is a Playground
Heavenly Muse: A Preface to Milton
Heavenly Herbs! Enjoy Them
Heavenly Soles: Extraordinary Twentieth-Century Shoes
Heaven's Flame: A Guidebook to Solar Cookers
Heaven's Tableland: The Dust Bowl Story

WHAT FAMOUS POPULAR SONGS MENTION HEAVEN?

The melody of "The Star-Spangled Banner" is taken from the music for "To Anacreon in Heaven," written by John Stafford Smith in about 1780.

Other "heavenly" songs include the classics "Pennies from Heaven" and "My Blue Heaven," as well as the more recent "Tears in Heaven" by Eric Clapton, and "Stairway to Heaven" by Led Zeppelin.

WHAT ARE SOME MOVIES AND PLAYS THAT MENTION HEAVEN?

Heaven Can Wait, with Warren Beatty (1978)
O, Heavenly Dog, with Chevy Chase (1980)
Pennies from Heaven, with Steve Martin (1981)
Days of Heaven, with Richard Gere (1978)
All that Heaven Allows, directed by Douglas Sirk (1955)
Rain from Heaven, written by S. N. Behrman (1934)

And, of course, there's Michael Cimino's *Heaven's Gate*— the movie that bankrupted United Artists.

WHAT IS THE MOST FAMOUS MOVIE ABOUT HEAVEN?

Probably Frank Capra's *It's a Wonderful Life*, with James Stewart and Donna Reed. This is the story of an angel who earns his wings by convincing a suicidal man that his life has meaning and importance to the people he's helped. It has been shown on television every Christmas season for almost three generations. For some families, watching it is an annual holiday ritual.

The story was adapted for television in 1977 and renamed *It Happened One Christmas*. It starred Marlo Thomas.

Scrooge (a retelling of Charles Dickens's "A Christmas Carol"), *Angels in America,* and three baseball stories—*Field of Dreams, Angels in the Outfield* and *Damn Yankees*—are some of the many recent popular works that deal in "heavenly" or "hellish" themes.

HOW IS HEAVEN DEPICTED IN MOVIES?

Movies usually picture heaven as starkly white, with fluffy clouds carpeting the floors. Everyone is dressed in white robes and speaks in hushed tones. In a significant departure, *Field of Dreams* depicts heaven as a baseball field.

In Jean-Paul Sartre's *No Exit,* hell is an empty room in which people needle and torment each other endlessly—leading to the famous realization that "hell is other people." In another clever interpretation, *Steambath,* hell is just that.

WHAT DO BUMPER STICKERS SAY ABOUT HEAVEN?

It seems almost un-American not to announce your beliefs on a car bumper. Here are some mobile thoughts about heaven:

Heaven: Good News for Bad Times.

Whoever Dies with the Most Toys Still Dies.

Don't Take Your Organs to Heaven. Heaven Knows We Need Them Here.

DO DRUG GANGS BELIEVE IN HEAVEN?

Apparently many do. A *New York Times* article about Los Solidos, a youth gang in Hartford, Connecticut, reveals that members pray at the beginning of meetings. One of the prayers asks God for help in carrying out gang duties, and includes the request: "If I die while on a mission, let me enter your kingdom in the sky." Members also take a religious oath to follow their leader to heaven.

WHAT ARE SOME AMUSING STORIES ABOUT HEAVEN?

Many vaudeville acts featured routines about heaven and hell, mostly about the latter and mostly unprintable. What follows are two printable jokes about heaven. Although some people might find them politically incorrect, consider that they are very old jokes!

A newly arrived soul approached the Pearly Gates and saw two lines of souls waiting to be processed. One line was very long; the other consisted of one lonely soul. Unsure of which line to stand on, the newcomer asked the last soul in the long line, "What are these two lines for?"

The soul answered, "This line is for husbands who were henpecked. That one is for those who weren't."

The newcomer, eager to meet a man who had not been

henpecked, floated over to the lone soul in the second line and asked, "What did you do to end up on this line?"

"I didn't do anything," he replied. "My wife told me to stand here."

On another occasion, a group of souls was patiently waiting in line to be admitted into heaven. Suddenly, a spirit in a white coat and carrying a stethoscope came rushing out of the Pearly Gates. He stopped along the line, taking pulses and checking heartbeats before rushing back in.

"What was that all about?" one soul asked an attending angel.

"Oh, that was God," replied the angel. "Sometimes he plays doctor."

In the spirit of equal time, here are two jokes about hell:

Having been judged in the Heavenly Court as just barely borderline, a soul was given the right to choose where to go, heaven or hell. Accordingly, the soul first made a tour of heaven, where he found stark white halls filled with hymn-singing angels. White-robed souls of the righteous dead sat in white pews, quietly singing or engaging in hushed conversation. Next, the soul visited hell, where he found people dancing, partying, sunning on the beach, and skiing on snow-covered mountains. Naturally, the soul chose hell.

After filling out the proper papers, the soul boarded the elevator, pressed the "down" button, and prepared for an eternity of partying. When the doors opened, two devils roughly dragged the soul from the elevator. The air was filled with tormented screams, and the stench of burning sulphur mixed with the chill of unbearable cold.

"This can't be right!" protested the soul. "I was just here and saw people dancing and partying and having a good a time!"

"Of course," said one of the devils. "You were a tourist then. Now you're a resident."

An elevator full of souls was going down to hell. At the first stop, the doors opened to reveal a room like a furnace, burning with white-hot flames. As the heat poured into the elevator, two souls were called by name and pushed into the furnace. At the next stop, the noxious smell of sulphur and brimstone greeted the remaining souls as several of their companions were thrown off the elevator. At the next stop, devils with pitchforks grabbed a few souls from the elevator and threw them into a giant pit of fiery serpents and burning oil. And so to the next, and the next, and the next—each stop more horrible than the one before. Finally, only one soul was left cowering in the elevator, fearfully awaiting his fate. The elevator stopped and the door slid open, revealing rolling green meadows, fields of wheat and corn, lush forests, and singing birds.

The elevator operator looked away in disgust, and said: "Damned Californians! Irrigating again."

CHAPTER SIXTEEN

HOW DO CHILDREN PICTURE HEAVEN?

Here are some actual quotes from children about their views of heaven.

Child viewing a manger scene:
"Is there electricity in heaven?"

Dinah, age 10:
"Life in heaven is like life here, only you don't get sick and die, and you don't have to work hard. You do all the things you like to do. There are lots of stuffed animals."

Child quoted in foreword to *Embraced by the Light*:
"I talked to Jesus and he was nice."

Joshua, age 5:
"In heaven I was a puppy. People patted me on the head. It was nice."

Dana, age 6:

"Before I was born I lived in Care-a-Lot. I played on the clouds with the Care Bears. When my Mommy needed me, I slid down the giant slide."

Child's note on memorial in South Carolina to two babies drowned by their mother:

"Dear Michael and Alex, I had a very good Christmas but in heaven I know yours was better."

Heather, age 6:

"Heaven is magic."

Jacqueline, age 6:

"There's no gravity in heaven. People don't stand on the floor. They stay in the air."

Beth, age 5:

"It's football and candy and picnics and dogs."

Jonathan, age 8:

"Heaven is a huge party that dead people go to."

Megan, age 5:

"Lots of clouds. They bowl, and that's why you hear thunder."

Matthew, age 7:

"Heaven is creepy because dead people are there."

Jeffrey, age 7:

"A very beautiful place ruled by God where kind dead people go and stay there for all the years the earth is alive."

Elina, age 8:
"In heaven rich people help give food to poor people."

Lindsey, age 7:
"A warm place up in the sky where people help God make decisions about the world."

Hillary, age 6:
"People get to look down at you and see if you're behaving."

Adam, age 8:
"It's way up in outer space. Everyone understands each other's languages."

Marni, age 5:
"They use flashlights for lightning."

Juliet, age 5:
"People get born again in heaven."

Jillian, age 6:
"People pick flowers."

Andrew, age 6:
"We get to see our parents again and talk to them."

Alexandra, age 5:
"People don't move because they're dead."

Benjamin, age 8:
"A nice place."

Shana, age 15:

"I don't think there's a 'fire' fire in hell. I picture it as sitting in a giant theater with thousands of people watching a movie of my life. And every time I do something really stupid, I burn up with embarrassment."

BIBLIOGRAPHY

Berthold, Fred, et al., eds. *Basic Sources of the Judeo-Christian Tradition*. Englewood Cliffs, NJ: Prentice-Hall, 1962.

Boni, Margaret Bradford. *The Fireside Book of Favorite American Songs*. New York: Simon and Schuster, 1952.

The Book of Mormon. Salt Lake City, Utah: The Church of Jesus Christ of Latter-Day Saints, 1976.

Charles, R.H., ed. *The Apocrypha and Pseudepigrapha of the Old Testament*. Oxford: The Clarendon Press, 1913.

Cox-Chapman, Mally. *The Case for Heaven: Near-Death Experiences as Evidence of the Afterlife*. New York: G.P. Putnam's Sons, 1995.

Eadie, Betty J. *Embraced by the Light*. Carson City, NV: Gold Leaf Press, 1992.

Eliade, Mircea, ed. *The Encyclopedia of Religion*. New York: Macmillan, 1987.

Encyclopedia Judaica. Jerusalem: Keter Publishing House, 1971.

Freeman, H., and Maurice Simon, eds. *Midrash Rabbah*. London: Soncino Press, 1939.

Galloway, A.D., ed. *Basic Readings in Theology*. London: George Allen & Unwin, 1964.

The Glorious Qur'an. Translated by Mohammed M. Pickthall. Des Plaines, IL: Library of Islam, 1994.

Graham, Billy. *Approaching Hoofbeats*. Waco, TX: Word Books, 1983.

The Great American Song Book. Dayton, OH: Lorenz Press, 1976.

Harder, Kelsie B. *Illustrated Dictionary of Place Names*. New York: Van Nostrand Reinhold Co., 1976.

Herford, R. Travers. *The Ethics of the Talmud: Sayings of the Fathers*. New York: Schocken Books, 1962.

Holy Bible: The King James Version. Baltimore: Ottenheimer Publishers, 1974.

Jacobs, Louis. *Jewish Mystical Testimonies.* New York: Schocken Books, 1976.

James, Montague Rhodes, trans. *The Apocryphal New Testament.* Oxford: The Clarendon Press, 1953.

John Paul II. *Crossing the Threshold of Hope.* Edited by Vittorio Messori, translated by Jenny McPhee and Martha McPhee. New York: Alfred A. Knopf, 1994.

Leiper, Maria and Henry W. Simon. *A Treasury of Hymns.* New York: Simon and Schuster, 1953.

Malz, Betty. *My Glimpse of Eternity.* Grand Rapids, MI: Chosen Books, 1977.

McDannell, Colleen, and Bernhard Lang. *Heaven: A History.* New Haven, CT: Yale University Press, 1988.

Meeks, Wayne A., ed. *The Writings of St. Paul.* New York: W. W. Norton & Company, 1972.

Minkoff, Harvey, ed. *Approaches to the Bible.* Washington, D.C.: Biblical Archaeology Society, 1994.

Moody, Raymond A. *Life After Life.* Toronto: Bantam Books, 1976.

Morse, Melvin. *Transformed by the Light.* New York: Villard Books, 1992.

New Catholic Encyclopedia. New York: McGraw-Hill, 1967.

Randles, Jenny, and Peter Hough. *The Afterlife: An Investigation into the Mysteries of Life After Death.* New York: Berkley Books, 1993.

Ritchie, George G. *Return to Tomorrow.* Grand Rapids, MI: Chosen Books, 1978.

Schouweiler, Tom. *Life After Death.* San Diego: Greenhaven Press, 1990.

Smith, Margaret. *The Way of the Mystics.* London: Sheldon Press, 1976.

Stewart, George R. *American Place-Names.* New York:

Oxford University Press, 1970.

Strong, James. *Strong's Exhaustive Concordance of the Bible.* World Bible Publishers, 1986.

Trickey-Bapty, Carolyn. *The Book of Angels: All Your Questions Answered.* Baltimore: Ottenheimer Publishers, 1994.

Van den Born, A. *Encyclopedic Dictionary of the Bible.* Translated by Louis F. Hartman. New York: McGraw-Hill, 1963.

Williams, John Alden, ed. *Islam.* New York: Washington Square Press, 1963.

ABOUT THE AUTHOR

Author Harvey Minkoff, Ph.D., is professor of English Linguistics at Hunter College of the City University of New York. A Bible scholar who knows Hebrew, Latin, and several other languages, he has published many articles about the language and literary structure of the Bible. Most recently he edited a two-volume work entitled *Approaches to the Bible*. This is his tenth book.